Concertina Maze:

The Michigan Review of Prisoner Creative Writing, Volume 9

M | LSA PRISON CREATIVE ARTS PROJECT
UNIVERSITY OF MICHIGAN

VOL. 9 – 2017

Printed by Dakota Avenue West Publishing, LLC

DAKOTA AVENUE WEST PUBLISHING

Detroit, Michigan

www.dakotavenuewest.com

Contents

Authors' Statements

Editor's Note

This year's volume is dedicated to our writer, our volunteer, and our brother Tim Hurley (1954-2016).

Acknowledgments

Thanks to the students and volunteers of the Editorial Committee and to my students in English 221, who voted on these pieces, corresponded with contributors and would-be contributors, and generally did most of the work; to the Michigan Department of Corrections, which allowed that work to take place; to Shon Norman of Dakota Avenue West, our printer, who is also responsible for layout; to everyone who submitted; and, especially, to Hannah Webster, Denise Dooley, and Leigh Sugar, without whom I could never have done this job.

Phil Christman

Poems

James Adrian
Did You Know Her?

She sat on couches with people who only wanted to exploit her pain
She burned dreams and electrocuted a past that she soon wanted to forget
She covered her head in storms and closed her eyes in hope to rid herself
of the Bogeyman
She could never be what everyone wanted or live up to the emotional bar
that kept getting higher
She's paying the price that was not affordable to most women despite the
hidden treasure she didn't know she possessed
She's spent many of moons being mentally raped by the overwhelming
tide of opinions eroding her self-confidence
She's muffled her screams that other women needed to hear because of
being taught that this is how it was back then
She's swallowed so much pride that it shows in her figure that can only be
approved by a man who's insecure & barbaric
She's ducked punches on the regular and been to the E.R. so much they
know her by name
She's suffered so much that her reflection only looks familiar through a
broken mirror
She's been harassed because of her private parts and made to feel inferior
in a world trapped in a bottle
She's been the face, the back bone, and the glue that held the family
together while putting her problems to the side
She wore an "S" under her dress all her life and it wasn't until it was too
late that I recognized who she really was… I'm sorry, Grandma.

Missie Alanis
Two Poems

Orlando

This is a Mickey Mouse Middle finger to
the Orlando killer; your God has always been
my God! You've only made God, more so "our"
God once and "for all,"
"For All," positivity remains
on call, the Midnight opens up
to the afternoon oil, for now those Angels never
have to cry human tears after relentless forge-
table toil. Oh My prayers have become a new drug
and your hate,
your repression,

My own prayer rug.
And after every Selah, I find dislocation and after
every "New Testament" you deal
me death and still I offer you a hug. And so we
will travel, not meet you halfway, but, come all
the way there on our own terms and conditions.

Feel what you haven't earned, love is the
only mission on our way there to your un-
opened arms we find a few "pet shops and the
Boys" soon after sing "Erasure," the girls are
dancing like Ellen, yellin' something about a
Colouurlesss Heaven
and 100/one hundred new wings; Halos with un-
Earthly bling and a before, during, and after-
math stonewall with a pulse, All Signal and
more alive than any pink love triangle, rain-
bows always find a will always find love in
the angle. Tillda Swinton, 50 dead, Tildaa
Swinnton, 50 dead, TTillda Swintton, 50
million watts, Meg, In the Cut
with my lover, Ryan, all of these things have and
will pass and I am living in the days when
Innocent is being killed, by words, before you even
have room to develop in the womb, I don't
need to assume that if my parents knew I was
Homo-unplannedus I would have

somehow came out blue and placed gently in a
trash can. And just think I never even had a
Chance to be brand new. I am "Living" in
the days when Innocence is being killed in the
pews, Don Lemon and Anderson have 360
degrees of awful, unwelcome news, Innocence
is being killed with religion, én levels, én mass.
If I had a big bank account I'd ask for a surgeon
and a tattoo artist to "open me up," so I could get
　　　　　　　　Orlando and Sandy Hook
tattooed on my heart where only I could look deep
within and see. "Some people want to die so they
can be free," but, The Purple om always knew
that, that outlook was a luster sort in Neva-
Neva land; propovall, God is "For All." So do-
n't fully stress, don't fully sleep until it's your time;
And that you should live free. why? 2nd in Comm and
Mrs. Annie Hall (Diane) said "Because I said so,
simply because you have to, it's what you've got
　　　　　　　　to do." And so I'm going to; I'm
going to continue to live under the light of all of
　　　　　　　　　　　　　　you.
And I pray I don't have to experience hate to-
day. Maybe I won't have to think or say "Fuck you,"
I can say "you know what; I love you," to a total stranger
and really solid gold mean it, That would
be nice because like a director of 40 plus films
the rest of the BS, I've scene it! Tillda Swinton,
50 Dead, Tilldda Swintonn, 50 Dead,
Tillda Swinton, 50 dead, Tillda swinton,
The Beach, The Box, The Saint, The Saint Con-
stantine, "Orlando," The female Marlin
Brando, killing her Gay Son's abusive lover,
　　　　　　　　another love undercover, electron-
ica thumpin' all in the club, down in Orlando,
　　　　　　　　the American down under, Just
her protecting the good ones. I wanna be like you
　　　　　　　　to all of them; A good Mum. Someone
on "The Deep End" of 49 continuances, I am the 50th,
the fiftieth victim. But, I will go all 50 distances
and until I am called home myself, all I can
　　　　　　　　really do (like you) is miss them.

Barbed Wire Bedtime Story

The stress of are you good enough: Are you good
enough? Over a few walls of wire, dire
desires to re-entry, the free world, envy, I have
      so much the less of plenty;
not a government worker, but, I work for the
      government, they sent me. My black-
ness works for the D.O.C. So they try to claim every
      single piece of me. Am I sicker than
a coughdrop, am I sicker than an IV with only germs
to drip, am I sicker than a doctor taking lives, am I
a statistic on the rise, then I close my eyes for
the moral of my own story. Once upon a time in a
land too close to lift the magick out of, too close for the magick
to yield faith. I found love that lead to my
imprisonment. Dual manifestations for more prolific
      than thee old ball and chain. My
Existence is all my spiritual accounts drained, the
essence of bankruptcy, this living afterlife has
made me one camel hump, survival at 125 degrees,
      Just you wait and see.
      Blue skies. Hold my mystical meadow
where not even one flower can grow. To full,
          flower
          flower

potential. And this one day the land closes in on
him and transformed every him into a her, and every
her into a him, what about then? A freelance tango.
Underground understanding was born for mature
audiences only. And everyone's soul was a conceptual
transplant, smart mold, silly puddy, acid
rain, muddy. Rediscovering new definitions of a
Heaven inside a windowless high rise. Underground tango
2, a movie unknown to Fandango but, a story so
true. And underground understanding became purpose
uncovering. Special places where even barbed wire
can transform into a vine of tender buds; uncolored new
          roses and thorns, in real time watch
it grow. But, if you never ask yourself am I good
enough to"live up to my own dreams," then you'll never know

Jennifer Avery
Hollow House

No one knows the roof that excretes blackness
as the clocks rotate counter-clockwise
sliced wrists have encountered a hatred ghost.

Visions once so full of color are devoured
by a warped mind twirling wickedly.

Now a pawn,
this mother is colliding between walls,
backed into corners she's coherent; no more.

Its name has its own house now
as flesh and blood drink an unavoidable silence.

It's a beast, blinded by a name when
mirrored images rape years in this space
I call "home."
The wiring in such rooms becomes destructible
to a toxic history.
Lanced, re-stitched like a pathogen un-known
to man.
I'm masked by statistics, I still thrive for
some substance.

Finally knowing God loves "me" even when I'm not "me";
now that's forgiven and free.

Charles G. Brooks, Sr.
Subjugation

If educAtion is the pinnacle, what, pray tell, is the base?
If it all starts at the bottom, racinG up on gossamer wings,
Then who officiatEs and by whose rules is the contest had?
My first wordly steps were feiNts, as I studied the mirage of choice—
Failed communities, leadership, dreams, sOciety
Looking for a hand; not up or down, just a stabilizing forCe,
Facing schemes plotted generatIons ago, just realizing fruition,
Conscientiousness setting in like fresh concrete on a midsummer's Day.
There is no escApe, no parallel universe; just us and no justice—
Not in a criminaL sense, but in a human sense—all lives matter.
Though it's stranGe that black lives are squandered mercilessly and
No retribution is justified, no restitution pAid, just harsh admonitions.
Indians have reservations and society gripes about that bequeathMent,
We lose schools in favor of sociEtal punishment.
Penal institutions, ne, correctional facilities, that don't correct;
They prevent the resurrection of sLavery, though slavery still lives,
Calculating my steps, running my race, lest I lose A foot on a mine
Or aN overseer's razor wire, forced to call myself anything but "Charles,"
A number instead oF a man.
Started from the bottom, and I'm still here, like mOst of us,
Useless, unless there's some menial task to be peRformed.
If education iS the pinnacle, racing Up gossamer wings,
Then who officiates and by whose Rules is the contest had?
Most importantly, who chooses the contEstants?

Demetrius Buckley
Two Poems

Something to Say

I made that letter out to you—my name & prison number—
everything needed to be on a stamped envelope. Travel-wise,
it will go through many hands before reaching yours,
hands of people love-struck for happy endings,
for grandeur, for low-lives becoming rich
from their newfound wealth & Kingship, their
stability. Nothing changes for us. I heard you have
two kids now & the guy you're with
—the one who blocks my calls—
is never around or left you after you were kicked out
on the street with a child on each breast; clothes
in garbage bags your oldest hauled
seven blocks to a urine stench bus bench
where you & your little ones stood
like herons nodding on a back of a crocodile. Waiting.
I knew then (and now) that my worries—the written kind—
would be in someone else's hand, tossed on a
coffee table with the rest of the mail;
but you—my physical kind—I didn't know
would be in the hands of another, splayed on someone's countertop,
easily read, your short clauses & phrases, his liking
then turning the page as he slowly thumbs through
with a gentle slide of a finger
while the envelope addressed to nowhere, to no one,
falls to the cold, expected floor.
Where do we go, then, when havens abscond
to the desolate depths of nostalgia? To self, I assume, to
the momentary collapse of dialogue,
to the ones who gave us up, left us with behavioral relapse
& practical repetitiveness to interpret
—to hell, I say, to hell with it all.

On the phone where we've been reminded
of being recorded, you tell me everything is fine
at home: your little girl can count up to sixty. I believe
the counting & fear the day my daughter
figures me out, the lie about me being an astronaut
in outer space, my blue-orange uniform

issued to the best pilot, always "Takin' off."
I think of something to say, begin fumbling through
the pile of unanswered letters that went
uninterrupted beyond the blank space of unansweredness.
Something to say: I will always love you, no matter what.

Letters from Daddy (7)

I never got the chance to tell stories
of how I made you, like how my father
used to tell stories—the colorful kinds—of how
he made me, put me together in his laboratory.
He would always begin in damp basement, him mixing
chemical in flask, Bunsen burner aflame, boiling,
then "Poof!" there I was, a reflection of elements
vibrating out of thin air. But as I grew more into the living
I began to head the story change, alter with each budding inch:
chemical meltdown in one, or too much flame
in another, but all the same configuration by his work,
his adjustment. With you, though, My Love, it was much more different,
ingenious, I would say, refined,
unique. I had no basement, no cylinder of flask
to hold the chemical, no fire. You were made
from particles that held the framework of worthiness & strife,
lattice of blood & spirit spewing across quiet rivers like
moonlight: beautiful. The flame—that shimmer in Mary's
unborn mist, that flick—was a miraculous spark
from an archangel's sword weighing transgression
on good & evil similar to our struggle, our carnal appetite
for iniquity. So in many words, I live for you in every
possible way to man, even when I'm not there with you.
Later in life you will evolve into woman, a flower
men will kill to uproot & display in vases, your hips catching every
stride, hooking onlookers, hypnotizing.
Your first lover will be unavailable,
translucent to what you give in the relationship; don't let it
change you, harden from clay that men grope
into their liking, cast a bold body of unshakableness
as you enter into womanhood, your power & if you
so happen to track down that road, that dry defying desert
full of dunes & dungeons, then travel light

when out a week of winter you're wearing sunglasses,
head down in compartment stores, terrified of mirrors.
Understand that it will hurt more to leave, to lie to yourself
saying you'll make it through those days
scratching down blackboards in classroom you gave up all;
realize that & run somewhere—anywhere—to singe the pain,
the thinking that a precious baby will bring him closer
to the idea of marriage; see him for what he is. Protect
yourself.

J. Rāheem Carswell
Struggling w/Existence, a Love Letter to the Orlando Nightclub Kidz

3:37 AM:
The bricks are speaking to me.
The discrimination & hardshipz of the Orlando kidz, keepz me up at
    night. The hate
                of someone'z gunz, materialize outta thin air.
The more I try, the more I crydown, my tearz are being taken—for
    granted.
So tonight I cut my fearz away, letting go of my last failure,
Compassionate breath that was never given to me.
Blood rain down my heart, causing me 2 be mesmerized by the fire,
Feel no pain from the stare, cause my smilez, stylez, and soulz—
Are gay. You go boo-boo kitty,
Hateful people who judge my sexuality w/a bullet,
Do I have civil rightz of freedom? Is this America or a—
Dictatorship of genocide w/people who look different in love.
Rebellious against your time, the colorz are a disguise,
My mask of shame… but why do I have to be ashamed of <u>me</u>?
You swim w/shame Bitch, see how far it getz you.
Patronizing facez encourage rage,
Power down and cry, it'll be easier this way, then the Orlando—
Nightclub kidz, can live in god's empathy, without fear of—
Oppressive hearts.

Humanz look at your identitiez az if they were your children
And surrender humanity's freedom.
It'z going to be alright Orlando, one day life will be different,
No bitternezz in your conscience spirit, your joy of singing w/
Lady Gaga will keep the mosquitoz away.

The world'z hugz will keep you warm, and pecan pie will—
Keep you sweet.
You were me, and I am you, you're not alone, and everyday—
I will listen 2 your heart.
            Holla,   J. Rāheem Carswell

John S. Copeman
The Moist Season (In the Penitentiary)

Sitting on top of these wet gray tiles,
trying to ignore everything including myself.
Can't help but notice it's all the same—
That I'm sliding across the slimy literary page of inadequacy;
as well as the sweating bathroom floor.
My shoes, which are dirty or walls that are deliberately short,
covering little more than intimate parts in public spaces.
Dropped paper rolls stick like thoughts,
wondering if Emily had the same problems?
Or could she write like that from Scotts in Huron Valley?
While summer in prison bakes just like Sylvia's oven, too.
The nerves that are frayed, over-crowded, the same.
Inmates mostly zombies coming at you, crisscrossing paths.
Moaning convicts sharing miseries, missing lives
they treated with utter contempt while still alive.
Measuring out my own life with Prufrock's coffee spoons.
As I am also pinned and wriggling on the wall;
slipping further down the mental road
they told me doesn't exist.
As an incarcerated veteran, No PTSD for you!
Without the "cakes or teas or ices."
Likewise not having the strength to force the moment to its crisis,
in short—I was also afraid.
Now I sit and watch the Perspiring Clock
drip strange time for us. Slowed down for those gone from the race,
but sped up for the highway crowds. Gasoline refugees going somewhere,
somewhere, somewhere they hope, but no where.
Just thinking that they are really moving on schedule.
Distracted with their plastic toys—heads bowed in free minutes.
The electronic worship at the temple of social media;
really caring about what strangers think of them.
Good citizens putting on pounds they didn't want
but can't seem to lose, like bad habits or bad news.
For those of us who watch and drool on shiny wet floors,
wishing we too could chew on the same fat calf,
or at least get some of the marrow reserved for their dogs.
While they heat up the planet with their unquenchable combustion
engines
and tell us it's normal to break summer records every summer.

Each year the water rising higher as the gaps in America
grow ever wider, like continents pushing apart.
So those of us at the very bottom gather our mops,
and put out the yellow fall'n man signs warning:
"Danger—Slippery When Wet," they say.
As we lift our feet against the indiscriminate tide.

* Inspired by T.S. Eliot's "The Love Song of Alfred J. Prufrock" (1915)

Kyle DA Daniel-Bey
Dear Society

Dear Society...
I want to thank all of you
for all the lessons you've taught
All the wisdom too
For the back breaking
baby killin
maiming, slayin, & raping too
For teaching us a place
not necessarily our place from which to view
the march of nations
of rampaging civilizations
How the strong eat the weak
& hell, even some of the strong too
You taught me not to trust
especially my own kind
While showing how progress can only
be gained w/ me & mine
Thank you for showing us
insanity can be survived
That a blood-shredded back was
for someone... a good time
Thank you for the babies raped into being
then stomped into oblivion
Mothers' stomachs slit while they scream & cry
as they hang from tree limbs.
Thank you for the men
servile & spineless crows named Jim
Who nevertheless rose up, time after time
& time again
Whose right to rule was a tool
of those w/ the lightest skin
Thank you for the show
w/o an ounce of substance
Thank you for the businesses looted
cahooted & burned to the ground
For the education w/o a place
at the table to make us proud
Thank you for the shacks
dilapidated hovels & projects

For the grassless yards, needle strewn parks
& dead end apartments
Thank you for the schools that fall
down around our ears
The books... oh the books
whose only truth is our tears
That tell your story & steals ours
w/o respect or fear
Those books, subject to the Texas Board of Education
yet haven't been renewed in years
Thank you for the system
that under the guise of education for all
Yet feeds our boys (& some girls)
into the penal system's voracious maw
Thank you again for the laws
those crooked as a broke-back snake laws
That w/o pause, exposes our flaws
& capitalizes on them w/o any just cause
That tells its stormtroopers that our lives
aren't worth anything at all
That tell young blonde school teachers that
our young men only want their draws
That equips its street gestapo w/ the latest
in military castoffs
Tanks & APCs, automatic rifles, vest & grenades
Night vision scopes for those dopes
who hang on roofs or even high up in trees
Thank you for the harshest lessons
those only to be learned in time
That our weaknesses & our strengths
you will turn to our eventual demise
That I should trust my own people
yet never trust my own kind
That if two of us get together
watch out for numbers 3, 4, or 5
That even my own momma will
w/ the right incentive, spit in my eye
That my father, like old Cronus,
will eat his own offspring, one at a time
I thank you for all these things
each cut, nick, & slice
For the knowledge that each imparts

& for the lessons that the truth bites
for forging us in the crucible
of your worldview & your fear
For making us accept some things
that couldn't have been made clearer
That you are our enemy
having been so from day zero
That we don't need a savior, messiah
or lone-gun-type hero
No, we are that foreordained
Ordained & sought light
That blade in the darkness
That slays ignorance with light
We are that salvation
bought & paid for in blood
So thank you dear society
You created what's about to come

James Galt
Wish Upon

I played dot-to-dot
With the stars
On a warm spring night,
Making a new constellation
By tracing the shape
Of your absence
In the distant, dark sky.

Then I filled the
Hollow inner space
With memories of you.

I made two wishes
As I closed my eyes:
For you, be happy;
For me, survive.

Monica Givens
Ghost

The ghost of you haunts me in the dead of the night,
Or on a busy walkway in the broad daylight…

Whispering, and taunting, and letting me know,
That you'll be there beside me wherever I go.

You're the scent in the air as the wind blows by,
Or the smile on the face of some random guy.

You're the giggle and laughter of an innocent child,
Or the breath of a lover that's frantic and wild.

You're inside me and with me, no matter what I do…
How can I forget when I'm haunted by you?

Yolanda Hobson
Teased

I've lied on people and said they raped me
Seeking attention I didn't seek
But it wasn't funny when I was charged with CSC 4th Degree
For the same lies I told on people
I've teased and beat drug addicts and homeless people too
It wasn't funny when I had nowhere to sleep
No food to eat, stuck on the corners robbing people
Stealing their cars for somewhere to sleep and heat

I called the CPS on my mother
And told lies
It wasn't funny when the CPS took my child out of my life
So now I'm missing out on his life
Because I chose to keep committing crimes and telling lies

I told lies and broke hearts
It wasn't funny when the first woman I've loved
Teased and disowned me and left me with a broken heart

If I can go back to the hand of time
I'll take every lie back
Love every homeless person
And help every addict
Because it's no fun when the rabbit's pointing the gun

If I could go back to the hand of time
I'll respect and appreciate my mother
Because now I know how it feels
My son is being raised without his biological mother
It's not funny, now the joke is on me and I'm being TEASED…

Ronald King Hood
Breathe

It was so horrific for us, not knowing whether our daughter would live or die. She was born two months premature… she was so tiny, and her lungs hadn't developed. Her heart was strong though. She was a fighter and she struggled to survive, to hold on.

I remember wishing for a boy when I first learned my wife was pregnant. I figured boys were strong and they would carry on the family name. But watching my daughter fight and struggle to breathe, I knew no boy would be strong enough to handle this. I could barely handle it. I'd thought so many times to just have the doctors pull the plug to stop my daughter's suffering. But it was as if she could read my mind, and her little heart would pulsate and beat faster, as if to say, "I'm here, don't give up on me."

Sixty-four days later, as my wife and I held each other tightly with tears in our eyes, the doctor unplugged the breather our daughter was connected to. She was breathing on her own, she had survived. We had survived.

Blaque Sheet Ja
Rebel in the Pleasure

Bitterness is my rival!
It's so hard to revel in happiness where every day is survival.
Where the wealthy are strong and the poor forgotten.
Where hearts tremble, and hope seems forever spoiled rotten...
And to the struggles of our compass, when will you lead us to our
So-called happy place?
If there so be one, can we be reserved a space?
What is the true difference between moral judgment and desperate
decisions?
Do we not know right when choosing wrong, but when nothing's right
We sin greater might I mention
Just to make peace the days of our lives.
Refusing to let our darkest nights conquer us, so there we strive!!!
What we fear should give ambition.
Through this jungle we step on vines of agony, and climb
Trees of trials, looking not for the grass that's greener; but the water that's
lighter.
Because we're born rebellions, and what they want us to dream.
We compel to differ and imagine higher!
We grow stronger the more they try to weaken us, grow
Ambitious the more they take from us.
Poverty and distress does not reside with trust!!!
So I say, bitterness is my rival...
But happiness is an enemy of mines, so call us friends.
(Dare To Rebel) The Roaming God
Protest Enemies Against Conquering Environments

Asia Johnson
Quis Separabit

Don't you love it
here? Love it here.
I need you
to run not away
but inside of here.
And lay here,
live here. Hedonism
is the way here.
You knew
the holding of my hand
meant the chaining of
your soul. But you dove
deeper. A believer
you became. Amens
and hallelujahs. Would
you just worship
and exalt it light candles
at the altar this
mattress latched to this
place you now call
home. And now the unknown
is anywhere outside of
me. Don't leave
from inside of me.
Don't breathe except
beside me.
"One does not leave
behind one's early loves;
they become part of one."
Part of me he is.
To not write
about him is to
renounce my namesake.
I am Asia, his
ex-girlfriend.
An amalgamation
of his semen
my pheromones. Stitched
through my fiber

is his skin. My insides
satiated with him.
Ridding myself
of him means
butchering my brain.
Unbinding means
dismembering my
body. Memories of
fateful days unburdening
him. Lonely nights
my co-conspirator and
savior a razor. A
means to an end
in my twisted
mind. Those nights
are my every night.
So no, I will do no further damage.
Seven years removed,
the apparition
lingers; dwelling
in the same part
of me that
stirs my writing.
My writing condemned
to his existence.
So here I sit.
Imprisoned.
Not composing
pieces about freedom,
flying, or the future.
But furiously dragging
this pen across
this paper. Praying
perhaps this time,
this piece will be
the piece that
separates me
                            from him.

Cameron Kelly
My Shadows

They walk endlessly
Through my mind
A thousand thoughts
A day
Thoughts I cannot leave behind.
My memories are my shadows
Always beside me
Never to be held again.

Bradford King
Dream

Days alive
    with song
Touch the night stars
Thistle down
    Riding on the wind
Serenity in a woodland pond
Benediction of the
    Setting sun
Dream of this beauty
Calming
    A troubled world

Patrick Kinney
Two Poems

You Want a Poem?

you want a poem?
then write one, sucker
don't just read
while the others suffer

don't just sit there
twiddling thumbs
pick up that pen
make fingers numb

go expound
on what you've found
turn off that TV
smash it now

smash your fist
into a brow
not others, but your own
that's how

smash it
till the words fall out
a metaphor, not really
ow!

are you slow
or just bereft?
you'll kill what brain cells
you've got left

you need a mind
to pen a verse
you need some sense
to make this work

you still believe
you want a poem?
then write one
this one's mine
and done

You (Still) Want a Poem?

Well, okay then
here you go
It may not be
what you hoped for though

It may not rhyme
or keep strict verse
and when you least expect it
worse!

Passive voice
who was—Oh, no!
clichés so, Katy,
bar the door

A little light alliteration
forc'ed metered rhymation
assonance so softly sung
as metaphorical bells are rung

And when end rhyme is not enough
we'll step out on a slant-rhyme bough
assault you with a nasal drone
or partially, like the common cold

A bit too long
abstruse and wrong
a sleep-inducing
freeverse bomb

Exploding words
pedantic turds
a Scrabble dictionary hearse

So when it's done you're left to wonder
who's to blame for such a blunder?
and who accepted that to publish?
I have shit-canned better rubbish

But, you know
whatever
So,
here's your poem
I've got to go

Ko
Advancement

Verse 1

All attractive supreme tactics are utilized./ And eventually mastered… and realized!/ On the corner spittin photons!/ Grain of rice tracking device./ Satellite's intercept rhymes./ Mass transporations… teleportation!/ Throw verses with eternal coordination./ Wiz pass NASA spaceships!/ Computer chips… up inside the rubber grips of lasers!/ X-rays without the strip search!/ Still in research!/ Discoverin… new elements!/ Finally addressin the… elephant… inside the room!/ Crafts hoverin… off of hydrogen and nuclear fuel!/ Transcendin… duality vision!/ Wholistic, universal mathematicians!/ Everything's a vibration, darkness almost endin!/ The Sun is revealed!/ Second comin ta build!/ With evangelist, atheist, and scientist, admirin bliss!/ Righteous requirements!/ The tyrant is… almost, ancient history!/ We can use him as compost… growth instantly!/ Also… we can hear the choir chantin… intergalactic!/ Travel through the cosmos to higher planets!/ For a vacation… amazement!/ Meetin different species, entities, and new races!/ New atmospheres!/ Inhale and exhale… life's a thousand earth years!/ Still hell!/ Network gear!/ The kingdom is here!/ Media communications virtual reality./ Telepathy!/ Brain cellys!/ Like Quatto!/ Humans mutating!/ What's the odds like Lotto… / to join who made me?/ Terminating biological reprogramming!/

Chorus

Advancin taking no chances!/ That's a law unrecognized… let's expand this… / better understandin!/ Leavin you stranded!/ So you all get left behind… by advancement!

Verse 2

Post-traumatic stress syndrome becomes post-ecstatic!/ Now pure service is automatic like drones!/ The globe… predicted to explode!/ Like Skynet!/ Metallic bones… high-tech satanic mindsets./ Super sex!/ Tantric trances is common practice!/ Steps to the everlastin… bypassin passion!/ Fashion in the immortal vessel!/ Artificial intelligence… like Johnny 5 some are disassembled!/ Bricks are bars of gold, bar codes, unknown cash!/ All credits… harum scarum, you can pass!/ Moonbases!/ Baldheaded like Sigourney Weaver./ Truth seekers… like excavations goin deeper!/ Either proper procedure or illegal search and seizure!/ By law enforcement or Feds./ A real life Judge Dred!/ Eyes blood red, blue beams, movin portraits!/ Mechanical obstacles… nature ran its courses!/

Heaven's office!/ CEO... Halo!/ Extraterrestrial!/ Professionals!/ Info superior... like the Predator!/ Competitors!/ Self identity dissolves like an Alka-Seltzer!/ As humanity evolves Mr. President's a military man!/ Fights in his own wars with comrades and cyborgs!/ Hope we can find the lord in due time!/ Movin through an illusion... it's similar to Tron!/ Freeze time!/ Usin cryogenics!/ Climb like Jacob's Ladder!/ Beyond matter and quantum physics... space bendin!/ Saints... clickin on your light within!/ God's electricians!/ In opposition to demonic assistants!

Chorus
Advancin taking no chances!/ That's a law unrecognized... let's expand this!/ Better understandin, leavin you stranded!/ So you all get left behind... by advancement!

Verse 3
Holy Legislators./ Councils, judges, and mayors... / convey to us data directly from the creator./ Just another day of recognition... spiritual cities!/ Submitting to the one before the beginning!/ No one in their right mind is risking.../ their well-being!/ For anything outside of the All-Seeing!/ In all places!/ Simultaneous occupation!/ No more grieving... transformation!/ Sound incarnations awaken!/ Like stimulation by the voice!/ For populations of androids!/ Calculations... by ethereals!/ Passed down to *Homo sapiens*... for a clearer view!/ Not mistaken for magnitude!/ Dialogue resumes between gods and men!/ The doctrines and laws begin!/ Written with divine pens/ Faster than the speed of wind and mind!/ Locomotive!/ Master and disciple like... Luke and Yoda!/ Authentic archdiocese reachin their quota!/ Pyramids on Mars!/ Solar ancestors being reborn!/ Fallen souls... the world reforms!/ Goin in... to a metamorphosis!/ Cities turn desert!/ Atomic missiles battle the feather!/ Christ!/ Remember me in paradise!/ The reservoir of pleasure!/ Hologram.../ my will before the afterlife!

Dell Koniecko
Two Poems

No Child Who Cries or Murders is Voiceless

No child who cries or murders is voiceless.

I wish I'd known sooner that lives depended on
my understanding this simple truth.
Perhaps I could have delivered my message to the world
in enraged diphthongs,
or used brutish syllables to quell the conflagration
that burned uncontrollably inside the too-young me.
With a weapon of words,
I could have fashioned a murderous phraseology,
and used it to begin the autobiography of a better man.
But what use are words now?
What language can raise the dead?

As a Captive She Swims Uncorrupted, but Alone

"We are very proud to have her here, because she is the only manta in
     captivity in the western hemisphere."
     —Spokesperson for Atlantis Resort in Nassau

As a captive she swims uncorrupted, but alone.

Great manta-wings that once propelled her perfectly through warm seas
now make small, graceful arcs on our conscience.
She knows that there are no queens in a pelagic sisterhood,
that they were all at risk,
and even now cannot hold a grudge.
While we appreciative beasts ooh and ah boastfully through the glass,
she isn't thinking of freedom or retribution—
only this: that the loneliness living in her
is a heavy price to pay for being more alive in her element
than we are in ours.

Randall Kuipers
Three Poems

A Cloud, 7 July

Opulent air
Lit from all light;
An expulsion of ice on blue.
Knotted fury, shade and spotlight ebb and ease.
I breathe.

Secrets

You gift me your words,
Deepest secrets to my ears.
They bleed from your trust.

Passage

All my calendars have no numbers.
Plenty of time
To do nothing, and
Anything,
But mostly shots of coffee—"two for three."
Creamer and creamer and sugar and hot, swirled
And blurry—
Distorted.
Broken, clockwise. It
Spinning, unwise. It
Has to
Break, and ballet, or it will sweep me under the rugged hands.
"I'll catch you at store, in four
Days."
But
Every day lasts forever.

*   *   *

The book I was reading—I forgot how she did that one thing;
I went back to read it, again, and it was easy for her to
Do it, again.

It was right there in front of me,
Then, and in her own time.
I tried to go back in my other book,
My
Other story, and the pages would not turn. Not that way. Could
Not turn.
Can't start over—move forward, move forward.

        *   *   *

I've misplaced some years—a necessity, I think;
Anesthesia enfolding me, but unable to address my temporal pain.
Every month lasts a fistful of hours.

Yesterday's game replayed this morning—
As if I wouldn't notice.
Tuesday's tickets, collected.
Wednesday's score, final.
Thursday's debts—paid.
Soup
Tonight.
But all my calendars have no days…

Tracy Leigh
Today's Enriching Plight

returned to the parking lot
   all the cars looked the same

continued searching for the earring
   accidentally knocked down the drain

morning sun that refuses to surface
   the heaviness as her heat hazes on

emergency phone call you're dying to make
   no recharge no range

veins in a leaf act as a spine
   once broken the leaf lay crumpled

dandelion fuzzy refusing to land
   examined intently for the inconspicuous seed

precedential periods in the middle of sentence
   beginning after the end

observe the profile in a quiet pond or
   the pebble that ripples it away

never-ending pages of her current book
   summed up in a sentence

the art of unrolling the toilet tissue
   without ripping it

a raindrop's journey ends on the window glass
   tomorrow remembered by its dustprint

Diana Lewis
Perception

Perception magnified
Eye of the beholder
    Hearts blazing a river of fire
    While others are smoldered
An enchanted dance
Of fire and ice
    The conclusion of chance
    Is the water—falling?
Or drying up in the heat? Of what U seek or
Of the SUN—* R U enticed
    365 Degrees, U & Me
    Where all we see
Is steel fences topped by barbed wire
And all white bricks
    Is it social disorder
    Caged by selfish desire or
A funeral pyre? Catching fire?
Ashes blowing in the wind
    Destruction of all the locked-away sins
    In and out, up and down
I wonder—
Do U see what's pulling me under?
I hear the sounds of lyrical thunder—
    Lightning strikes a powerful blast
    This too will come to pass
Cloudbursts release falling rain
You can grow new life
    Or enhance your pain
    Attitude
Strong state of mind
Perception personified
    When U stand 4 something strong
    It will stand 4 U
A real leader has heart and follows
Their inner truth—
    Perception misguided
    Dissed, missed, dice rolled, cards fold
A gambler's infatuation
As your legacy is sold, my bad told

What's your motivation?
   We need 2 stop playing roles
And transform—
From the norm
   Uniqueness is a thunderous strength
   Control a devious rank
Perception—
Like so many small stones on the ground
Many different colors and shapes
   Coming together to form a foundation
   Not to placate
Or replicate
But 2 shine individually
   For their difference yet be equal
   That makes perception an equal opportunity
REALITY
Not a fatality!
   What's your PERCEPTION?

Alex Lockhart
Black Bananas

Even discriminating welfare mothers
could not be blamed for eschewing
the sad sacks of bruised tomatoes
of Walmart's dubious produce section
The poorest of Bridge Card shoppers
in big-box birdcages
would reject a pest-infested stalk of
cauliflower or quarts of curdled milk
Would a sensible consumer volunteer
to advocate for rotten avocados
what with their splotchy rinds wilting
from their humiliating humid existences

So surmise my surprise
when I realized the graciousness
of altruism
Those who selflessly forfeit their
precious leisure days to enter a
concertina maze of electrified teeth
Enduring the indignity of an unpaid
phase of metal detection procedures
and contraband sweeps inside
their mouths and beneath their feet

Is this a degradation worth their salt
Do tears ever abrade against the grain
of a thankless morale
Does it ever taste like consuming
spoiled fruit to
patronize pariahs like Calcutta
lepers littering the landscape with
lost limbs for someone else to come
behind and clean up.

Your integrity and resolve is moving
The courage you wear like a thick peel
to foster us like Syrian refugees
despite our seedy and grubby deeds

You could be swimming in sunlight and
white sands of pure Lake Michigan shores
with children and aquamarine weekends
Your interest disillusions my skepticism
That, of your own accord,
you'd donate yourselves to mentor
some socially crooked miscreants

But a fruitless chore is not yours
At least not in this All-American
profitable institution
I'm beholden for your effort,
others are too,
for the revolutions we receive
around the crystal face of
your timepiece
For your head pledge and heart space
Your attempt to vitalize the fruit
languishing on the vine, the wormy
apple that others avoid

Before my childhood perished
like a sere toddler in a hot car,
my mother stayed my intent
to dispose of a hand of
overripe blackened bananas
She transformed the soft fruit flesh
into a moist baked loaf of
flavorful banana bread instead

She saw value in what otherwise
appeared to be decaying refuse

Not unlike my appreciation
for her capacity to see veracity in the dregs
I'm consoled and impassioned
by your generosity and compassion
Your measures haven't gone unrewarded
My recompense for your diligence—
I will endeavor to be the best
loaf of banana bread I can be

Kyree Lyn
True Obsession

As I sit upon the wall
I tend to smile down on you
My hands waving at you
As time passes by
Minute by minute
Hour by hour
I sit and watch
Tick tock, tick tock
I see you watching me
Always looking my way
I am your constant obsession
I always seem to take your gaze
Minute by minute
Hour by hour
I sit and watch
Tick tock, tick tock
I soon come to realize
It's not me you're after
You're after what I can give you
You're after my time
Minute by minute
Hour by hour
I sit and watch
Tick tock, tick tock
But won't you be sad
When my life runs out
And I can't give you
What you want
Minute by minute
Hour by hour
I sit and watch
Tick tock, tick tock
Soon enough time will stop
My batteries will run dry
I hope you have a big supply
To keep me alive
Minute by minute
Hour by hour
I sit and watch

Tick tock, tick tock
Time seems to slip by slowly at first
Then faster and faster
Until everything comes to an end
Time always ends in death
Minute by minute
Hour by hour
I sit and watch
Tick tock, tick tock

Paul McNee
Rock Star

Birth
Toy
School
Guitar
Stage
World
Dope
Death

Jill Miller
Where I am From

I am from Nebraska,
land of corn and football.
I am from family and closeness,
from being on time
and, "watch where you're going so you don't fall."
I am from the leaf-drenched trees,
the cut grass,
from the smell of gasoline and diesel,
from playing in the dirt
and always making the call.
I am from when pen meets paper,
from numbers and words,
from punctuation and meaning,
and, "Hi ya'll."
I am from the look and the stares,
from the before and the after,
and having it all.
I am from fingers and hands,
from helping and giving,
from cooking and baking,
from the chicken noodle soup,
And, "it's okay if you fall."
I am from the shade under the trees,
the long, deep discussions,
from learning new things,
and shopping at the mall.
I am from learning to drive a stick in the rain,
from the dirt roads,
from the cornfields with friends,
from "lover's lane," from "seven sisters,"
and remembering it all.
I am from the birds and fears instilled,
from animals and the smiles,
and wanting to play ball.
I am from snow-skiing and soreness,
from laughing until it hurts,
from making new friends,
and my collections of dolls.

I am from riding my bike all through town,
from going to Walt's after the game,
From cruising main,
and driving around with them all.
I am from holidays and gifts,
from playing games,
from being surrounded by family,
and giving them my all.
I am from boats and jet skis,
from the water and the docks,
from the stars and the moon,
and getting lost in them all.
I am from death and loss,
from hurting and sorrow,
tears, and smiles,
from turning bad into good,
and missing them all.
I am from creating those four sets of eyes,
from family.
I am from Steve and DelRae,
who always gave me their all.
I am from head to toe,
a girl—that's all.

Justin Monson
The Little Death Sestina

Oh, he caught some chest shots
He didn't make it... but I don't know
Nothin' about all that, he says of the guy he killed.
Casual as the ordering of a sandwich, play-by-play of a sport
I've not played. A man my age murdered over frictioned skin
At a birthday party. War stories wane, we separate, I read a book until
     sleep

Strikes against day and I dream of light matters. In my sleep
I remember the beach in Port Huron, horizon throwing shots
Of thin clouds across empty space: fingers reaching for warm skin.
Tide froth laps on our little piggies letting an entire generation know
The lion's share of time we opt to sport
Shoes will become millennia detached, eventually innocence killed.

I rise with dry mouth and swat the air: mammoth fly killed.
Pancaked into the garbage no farewells from friends. Do flies sleep?
Imagine a Papa Fly throwing tiny baseballs to his son, saying *Hey sport,*
You haven't tried pop flys yet! Why don't we give it a few shots?
The kid fly says *Ehh... I don't know, Pop. I don't know...*
Can't I just hang out with my friends on that guy's skin?

Imagine Papa Fly weeps on the wall after I've shut down the party on my
     skin,
His son killed.
By a being he can never know.
New meaning now given to *fly on the wall* only minutes after my sleep.
Maybe Papa Fly goes to the Fly Pub and downs shots
Of fermented sugar droplets and watches ESPN replays of some sport

He doesn't even know the rules to. He thinks *What a dumb fucking sport,*
As he orders tiny Buffalo wings then pulls off the orange skin
Of each wing but decides he has no appetite. *More shots!*
He screams, sobbing into his plate of naked wings, his son killed.
I am wondering now if I've gotten enough sleep
Because it seems I've lost my mind and I don't know

Where to find it. Over the last five years things I know
Have become finger clouds over lush grounds where the sport

Of time plays on and on and on until we forever sleep.
I felt nothing when he told me of bullets through skin.
By now I've heard it a million times, men being killed.
Like ordering espresso, he spoke of the shots

Fired into a man I know by degrees and I sport those shots.
They swirl around in my head: a beautiful concerto of killed
Innocence with sleep deprivation, a development of armored skin.

Gregory Richard Mox
Blue-Gray Eyes Senn

Let the Universe serve as your Bible
And look to the whole of Creation
For the character of the Creator.
Is there such a being?
Or did All-That-Is erupt from blind Chaos?
Are such questions just human-scale foolishness,
Products of finite minds confronting infinity?

So look upon the Universe
For what can be learned.
If the Creation is babbling nonsense
Then blind Chaos is the Creator
And so be it.
But if Creation has some guidance
Then infer a Creator wishing to guide
And so be it.

The Universe is inhumanly vast
By which the Creator states,
"I am beyond your scope."
The Universe is very nearly empty,
By which the Creator states,
"Look well at the deep skies
And know that life is a rarity
And what is so rare is precious."

The Universe is slowly dying.
By which the Creator states,
"Death is the price of living."
The Universe is alight with beauty,
By which the Creator states,
"Life is worth that price."

The setting Sun's beauty is humanly vast,
By which the creator states,
"Death is not to be feared."
Why else should a Sunset so move us?
Science cannot answer that
Not can science explain why

Those of us who cannot dream
Must soon die.

The Creation does not babble nonsense
And blind Chaos explains naught
So the Creation is art
And our Creator is the artist...
What need is there for an afterlife?

An afterlife seems a peculiar idea,
For after life comes death,
That's what those words mean.
But we have been thoughts
In the mind of our Creator
And that is eternity enough.

If something after should there be
Then all the better is life,
But the Creation is art
And our Creator is the artist...
So we are honored beyond words
Just to be parts of such work.
Leave Creation better
For you having been
And reply thus to our Creator.

JaMal Sam
The New Iron Age

Iron sharpens Iron, and I see no glass
Only essential tools in building our future.
Did Dr. King not convince us to be "free at last"?

We respectfully give thanks to the strength in our past
Rather bleed for our Motherland than surrender and lose her.
Iron sharpens Iron, and I see No glass.

Only constructive efforts applying pavement to our path.
A foundation of Unity instead of mindless shooters
We hold value in each other, not a fist full of cash.

An example for our community where blood stains the grass
Blood stains the legacy of our ancestral Rulers.
Iron sharpens Iron, and I see NO Glass.

GOD created us to love us, so love the us that we have.
Our struggle is only that should we neglect to be tutors
A foundation of Unity, essential tools in our future.

Presenting light to opposing forces prepared for a clash.
As we Unite to stand firm, not one to maneuver.
Iron sharpens Iron, and I see **NO Glass.**
Did Dr. King not convince us to be "Free at Last"?

Michael Sullivan
scumocracy

the evil few
often rule
trying to be somebody
eternal pissants
whose bite is infected by the
pain and suffering they cause
(such is their eternal glory)
they clump together
a floating cover of slime
doing evil
telling lies
calling it good
sad but true
scumocracy

Robert Tiran
An Expansion of Charles Bernstein's "Frequently Unasked Questions"

"I've a pile of memories on my other" shelf
  the one behind my desk,
  due west of that night-light.
They're in that jar, up high
  reminding me
  what fears
  what lies
  what little truths
  crafted me.
The lid is tight
  no air
  no sound.
But yes, that's them loudly screaming,
  yet not from mouths.
I've considered setting them free… although
  they seem at home in their jar
  on that due west self.
Screaming at me.

Karmyn Valentine
In Stillness

"How much of the self is skin?"
who is more naked
once houses are drawn
you can draw on elysium's
still grasses, dancing oaks
ahead years still unknown

in the book of things
a corpse's dialogue still silent
still voice still mirror still inside

no requiem

such is the acoustics of sadness
you stand and you're still there
I am still writing for you

such is the ache of counted words
sense of sound attuned
silent if not for trees

greater heights
so greater the falls
kindling for my sheds

pines raise wires carries words
cemeteries cap my skull where not a reed grows
but floods, in ashes

waters humbled by stones
the measure of a note that is no note
thought is sodden is rule is broken
halves release cables
I ran left, I lay down

    I lay down.

G WAHID
Ask Yourself

What are you looking for?
Can you see?
Oh you want the best right!
What will that be?
Are you prepared to receive that which you desire?
Would you be mad when life tests you and call you higher?
Pulling you closer to the things you really seek!

Have you analyzed yourself lately?
Questioning your every move!
Your every thought!
Being careful of the words you articulate!
Have you found yourself?
What is your true self?
Have you ever lost yourself?
In order to regain yourself in the most authentic way?
Do you understand that your future starts here today?
This is a new beginning, a new start.

Ask yourself, are you ready?
If not this is your time to get ready.
Are you scared to obtain the things you once saw?
Your vision, goals, and dreams!
Is so move forward, let go.
Eradicate every negative emotion holding you back,
Separate yourself from those people, places, and things, that's stagnate.
Think about what you really want, be confident and your mind will attract
it.
How's that you say?
Well that's the law of attraction, gravitating those things to you which you secretly
desire.

Ask yourself are you a quitter or are you a fighter?
When adversity come your way fight harder?
When it's easy to give up or give in think smarter.
Anything worth having you should work for it, as well as be patient.

Ask yourself if quick fixes last long?
Or do they satisfy your immediate needs then pass on!

Charles Washington
Little Lost Boy (When will I see you again?)

Little Lost Boy, I haven't got a clue,
of when I'm coming home, so I guess it's up to you
to grow up and be, the best that you can be
and not end up like your father: me!
You see, I've always promised that I would never leave you
now deep in my heart I feel like I've deceived you
I never thought about the rules of the system
now I'm giving you wisdom from inside of a prison
I wonder how many days you walked to school by yourself?
My presence is gone so you look to someone else
to fulfill your needs and the space of your father
but then you say to yourself, "He don't care, so why bother?"
Daddy is gone and you start to accept it
You're feeling neglected so it's only expected
that when you grow up you will start to resent me
I can't think but the worst, and the feeling is chilling me
I can't tuck you in when you lay down
I can't pick you up when you fall to the ground
All I have is memories; photos of you and me
I pray to God everyday that it will be like it used to be:
like laying in our living room, watching music videos;
dressing you up real warm when it was cold;
and how I followed you around outside as you played
every time I reminisce it only saddens up my day
What school do you go to? Who are you friends?
How does your day start? How does it end?
Those are the questions that stay on my mind
I searched for the answers but they're too hard to find
I always wondered if you'd like the same things that I like
I never had a chance to buy you a shiny new bike
and take off the training wheels, and teach you how to ride it
I know you're still very young, but please pay close attention;
try hard to prosper in life's every mission
'cause I did this to myself, I can't blame nobody else
The strongest man in the world can't take the pain that I've felt
Without you and your sisters, I'd probably think of suicide
I don't want to die, but why stay alive?
If I can't be with you? 'cause all I do is miss you
It's a sensitive issue, I want to hold you and kiss you

but when I come home you will probably be a senior
Live by spiritual values and give God all the glory
there's just no way you'll ever know the full story
of how when your grandmamma needed me, I failed to protect her
so God took her away because I didn't respect her
I know right now that you can't fully understand it
but I'm a six-digit number; to society I'm branded
When I first left, you were only three
now you're eighteen; imagine what that does to me
Damn how it hurts being torn apart
I don't mind being broke, but I hate a broken heart
I wonder what it would have been like to watch you grow?
I guess you and I will never know
I'll never forget how we played in your room
or Saturday mornings watching your favorite cartoons
It hurts so bad for you and I to be torn
the picture is vivid of the day you were born:
seven pounds and fourteen ounces is what you weighed
December 25th is your birthday
you are the best gift in the world, you brought me so much joy
I don't want to see you be another lost boy
'cause we are a team, meant to stay together
I hope this separation won't last forever
With you and your sisters is where I belong
until I'm with you again, please Chachie, be strong
Little Lost Boy, what I say is true
if you only knew, just how much I need you
then you would forgive me, and so would the others
your mama said she wouldn't wait for me, but I still love her
Little Lost Boy, so very, very lost
I really need to be with you, even at all cost
'cause you are my son, and you are my best friend
Little Lost Boy when will I see you again?

Cozine Welch
Six Poems

Sunderland Street

A Sunderland Street
where my grandmother stayed
who's to say whether or not if
on that day that I remember most
who's to say that I hadn't,
that sublimely unblemished Self, I,
who's to say that I hadn't
just then
come back into my awareness of the present moment
at the exact moment
having previously put myself on
earthly automatic
daydreaming, as some would have it,
abstracted / distracted
gone intergalactic into the ascendant
attic of the mind
of space and time
so that I could get a better feel for
this elastic fabric that our
pattern has been
woven from
putting my Self on earthly automatic until
my chauffeur double-parked my avatar
my park-assist partly pissed
argument ensuring a
well placed threat threw in and
I had to crawl back
down, into, outside of
and up to a
Sunderland Street
where my grandmother stayed
because my face was bleeding
and a voice was
screaming
from my throat
my vision colored red
blood
brimming with tears

the scene I recall
from the day that I remember most
orbiting around my spinning vision
practiced detachment rendered
defenseless
against this
shock transmuting sweat into cement
limbs locked
heart racing free in wild arrhythmia
What happened?   She said

I don't know
I don't know

Sobeit

A backalley
    in a backwater
A backstroke
    in time
back, again
i once asked a man
what space is made of
he said time
large alcoholic arms sweeping
hyperbole to emphasize
hyperbola
watery eyes bloodshot
vessels forked like
arcs in a plasma globe
Can't you see? It's all
time!
time
how much time separates us
now
me from you?
how much time is traversable?
it seems none
where i am
always so far from
where I am

from
where i want to be
a tide that never comes in
always lapping up
upon a distant shore… *gate, gate, paragate*

40 Million Xs

I'm the Xs in the dictionary
brief, often overlooked and
easy to pass by, to skip
past, but exotic and
exciting when found, fulfilling and fetishized for
a moment, passé afterwards
two pages out of 1,600
a percentage not even
worth the equation, not worth
the mention, or
something like a something something—not even worth the metaphor
perfect?
no
body
think about it
perfection?
every
body
what is there to think about?   from
400,000 (slaves)   to
40 million (african-americans)   over
400 (years)
give or take
and still I feel like
I'm the Xs in the dictionary

It Takes One To

He didn't know what the fuck
obdurate meant. Liar
sitting at my table stringing
nonsensical noises together insync

with the stuttered nods of sycophants
obsequious in 7/8 time
my face is obfuscated
made so
to match my plainclothes detective demeanor
I'm cool. Yeah,
hey man, don't mind me
I always look like this
nose and eyebrows pinched
conjoined as if
I can smell your bullshit.

Never-born (a song for him)

A chance of rain with pain in the forecast
a letter come slide under my door

Tear stains on the page where she wrote last

what is she so sorry for?

Well, seems me and my baby had a baby
but that baby ain't a baby no more

It's too many years she'd be waiting
I'm facing Life plus 40 years more

She say: You know it ain't right to raise a lil' lad
when he ain't never gon' see his dad except
through pictures framed in glass

Yeah, yeah, if truth is truth then I can't be mad
maybe it was too much to ask that
you not just decide that on your own
and leave me here to mourn

My boy was never-born
My boy is never-born
My boy was never-born
My boy's never-born

So I pray: Hmm, God bless the dead
keep and protect every hair on his head

may he
have all the strength of his dear old dad
but the kind disposition of his mother instead
may he
keep hopeful when things go bad
and not worry when he can't,
but do all that he can and since we
can't keep him sheltered safe in our hands
may he be born into the arms of
someone who can, Lord

and who knows...

Maybe babies get a chance to choose
and maybe, baby, you'll forgive what we do
and when the time comes
you'll come and find us
and baby, I promise
          we're gonna love you
          Oh, we're gon-na love you

I'm sorry, baby
So sorry, baby
I'm sorry, baby
We're sorry, baby

So Easy A Caveman

I should learn to paint instead
I should learn how to
transubstantiate (yeah, that's it) mental visions into
physical image
to play with optical dimensions
to cleverly allude to 3
where only 2 exist
do visual artists often feel as
off-the-mark as I
often do
your technique telling of
your limitations
finished product not leaving you as
awestruck

as inspiration had promised

Something gets lost in translation when
idea
gathers material
clothes itself in comprehension
and is bound by the chains of language
imprisoned by intellect
spiritual speech turn weak matter slave
of a lower vibratory rate that
came
gave itself into bondage
at the promise of becoming
a created thing
of beauty
only to be
left empty in a vacuum-void of
impotent impact

I am a Cro-Magnon
trying to describe a phantasm
whoo-oh. Uh. Uh!
Stuck
idiot-hit
numb-noggin'd
Dumbstruck.

Calvin Westerfield
Shades of White

White is the color of the rising sun
Whose light reveals a Brown fetus thrown in the trash.
Infanticide rooted in pride; a Black mother
Stolen from her tribe and sold, had to decide
If she would bear a foreign seed,
Forced inside her the same night she was bought,
By a pallid monster proclaiming rape as his right…

White is the report of a pig's discharged gun,
Aimed at the back of a Black unarmed teen,
Who was afraid for his life and chose to run—
Slain at point-blank range while trying to flee
The scene of a murder before it occurred.
Nine shots were heard a mile away, but
Today this pig roams free; a jury
Of his peers found him not guilty…

White is the stench of Africa's son, swinging
By his Brown neck from an old poplar tree;
Rigor mortis set in. Accused of having been heard
Rousing the minds of fellow slaves with thoughts of being "free."
Death squeezed the hearts of his wife and daughter,
Tighter than that tattered noose that took his life.
White is suffering, pain, and strife on the loose…

White is the taste of tears on the face
Of an incarcerated Black man sitting on death row,
Wrongfully convicted for the rape and murder of Jane Doe.
Appeals exhausted to no avail. 20 years in a single cell,
Feeling out of place. Mind full of affliction;
Despite his good diction, he finds hate in his heart
He can't express. The execution is in ten hours,
But he won't request a special meal, confess, or
Say any last words before he's killed…

White is the feel of cotton on the bruised
Hands of an adolescent field slave.
Having labored twelve hours, he gave the ofay a full sack.
White is the pain of 30 lashes to his Brown back,

For his sack being 30 pounds light. Between the
Lacerated flesh was white, as he lay bleeding on
His rucksack, open wounds exposed to the night,
In an attempt to recoup for the coming day;
Agony steals his sleep, so he decides to pray
To a white god in the sky. Not yet twelve,
But ready to die. "Master" will place a tiny white
Cross on his grave—a white burial for his
     Conquered Black slave...

Moses Whitepig
The Toy Box

When we are young, we love to play with toys, pretending to be grown-ups.   We all seek to manipulate the illusion.

As children, it is easy to guide the world in a manner that suits us. We are given a miniaturized world, in material form, in order to organize it on an exoteric level in imitation.

As children develop, the perceptions of separated existences impose limitations on the ability to order the world to their will. The powers of ignorance become greater and the agreed-upon reality becomes the norm. Yet, we still want to play with toys. We still seek to manipulate the illusion.

The toys of our miniaturized play become larger and more powerful. But they are still the toys of childhood.

We become drawn into the deception until it becomes inescapable.

Our toy box becomes a death trap of our own design and we are blind to the fact that it is all a game of "let's pretend."

Desmond Williams
PEOPLE vs. A.K.A.

Never had a shot, the sirens never seem to stop, in the middle of the
night you could hear the guns pop, my reality the streets would watch
me bleed, my life under siege, by a system that won't let me breathe, the
air I need, suffocated by the people that supposed to protect me from
these streets, but instead wants to see me six-feet deep, categorize; to be
a victim or commit a homicide, stacked against me is political lies, that
keep me confined, long enough to plot a political crime, now I'm faced
with political time, and no one on the jury is peers of mines, judged by
an upper class, here's a news flash, they only show and report the bad,
what about the kids that show up for class, or the single mom that work
a doubles for what she has, they're scared to show your success, rather
see me with a gat, or in a hearse stretched out in the back, only C.S.I can
picture that, let's face the facts, was I ever supposed to make it out with all
those holes and cracks, some of us fell through, beat the odds after seeing
what hell could do, profiled; let that sit and marinate for awhile, picked
out of a crowd, because of my racial style, a two-day jury trial, the system
done handcuff another Black Child, the cycle of life, it's like a worthless
fight because I'm the only one that seem to know miranda is white.

Fred Williams
These Images

Those flowers out front/ are just a front
those flowers out front are like   mascara on a monster
those shallow-rooted flowers buried on top of generations of
brutality and cruelty
my
inexpressible inflammation that the flowers out front can
put a smile on people's faces disgraces the prisoner that
planted them

planted the misconception that this hell is   home
some people are alive with no purpose
dead above the surface
worthless with no self-determination/

they give you flowers when you're dead but no soup when
you're sick/ sickening confusion/ that the vibrant, pretty,
colorful flowers can overshadow the darkness
that this place has taken what is ours/

our mothers/ our sons/ our fathers
those flowers are a contradiction/
the disarticulated stems disjointed/ submerged in dead soil/

those flowers out front/
where
tombstones should be

those birds and bees are not supposed to be here
reproduction in a cemetery is oxymoronic, paradoxical and
incongruous/
the genocide and suicide in this place can't be misplaced
by well-placed tulips, lilies, dandelions and your damned
lies! Those flowers out front should be black roses.

Amber Wilson
Living in Hell

How does it begin?
For me, it didn't start with sin.
I took a different pathway in,
To end the game that no one wins.

Now I'm just a looney trapped in a cage—
Helpless,
Enraged,
Afraid,
Screaming in pain.
Things simply happening.
No freewill;
Just destiny.
I'm screwed up in ways you wouldn't believe.

At times I can see,
But sometimes they're blinding,
The evil rings circling.
Never-ending, this seems…

I keep trying to understand,
I'm really part of a cosmic plan.
But faith doesn't carry weight,
Some days,
When I can't shake the blaze.

Here now remembering things,
Things sick and tormenting.
I'm fighting to get my mind free.
Maybe I'll achieve,
Eternal peace and harmony.
If I can manage to kick this disease.

So heinous and cruel,
Is suffering the fools,
Who lie over truth to avoid having to do.
Instead they just use,
Whatever they can accrue,
Until they strangle to death in a hedonistic noose.

But there's pleasure in Hell,
Any psychopath will tell:
Self-hatred that compels the cheap ones to sell,
Their soul to rebel,
Against anything well.
They enjoy fiery reign, the infidels.

So in searching for an answer,
To rid the world of human cancers,
I'm getting fucked by a wicked master—
Exploring Hell in the darkest chapter.
Brain spattered,
And life tattered.
I'm stuck in an existence that to me no longer matters.

And day to day I notice things change,
And it relieves me of some of my pain.
Yet what's insane,
All that's past remains,
And I'm burnt all over again.

The only consolation made,
For this life beyond the grave proclaims:
Who I am won't go away—
The beast will never take my name...
But this comforts me in vain

I want my life to not be fucked.
I want my mind the way it was,
Before I ventured through the sludge,
To know what evil really does.

So here I wait,
Imploring Fate,
To free me from the cage of waste;
'Cause my life's a game,
And on this stage,
I don't get to set the pace.

I wish and pray that soon someday,
My true and handsome sage, I'll face,
And he'll save this weary slave...

But as I say,
That's not the way
Things work inside the flame.

Instead, I'll say,
Until the day,
The map to Satan's through is made—
Destroying escape,
From negligence's shame,
(Which all demons hide with lies and pain).
Then no more will Hell remain.

Greg Winer
How Fortunate a Snowflake Is

How fortunate a snowflake is,
A child of destiny—
Sent from heaven, dressed in white,
Arriving silently.

Like skillful tiny seamstresses,
They gather on your bed—
Then stitch a quilt to blanket you,
From winter months ahead.

When robin brings her springtime song,
With golden notes of sun—
The warm breeze blows the covers back,
Undoing all they've done.

Into the ground, they trickle down,
And drip upon your lips—
A kiss each spring—I can but dream,
How fortunate a snowflake is.

Prose

Craig Benson
I Told You So!

Attention! This is not a test! This is an alert of the Emergency Broadcast System for the Greater Yellowstone Area. The Yellowstone Pass Police Department has issued a shelter-in-place order, effective until 12 p.m. tomorrow. If you should encounter a chicken at any time, DO NOT APPROACH. Take cover and immediately contact the Greater Yellowstone Sheriff's Department at 555-674-1235. This has been an alert of the Emergency Broadcast System.

We now bring you a Super Duper Action News Four Special Report. Here's Craig Benson: "Good evening, Yellowstone Pass. It is with a heavy heart that I bring you this tragic report concerning a long-thought wives' tale. In an attempt to bring clarity to this outbreak, it is my pleasure to introduce Doctor Dingledorph Chickenspear Professor of Intradimensional Horizon Walking at Northeast Polytechnic State University. Professor."

"While I would love to sit here today and say 'I told you so,' I will use this forum to educate you simpletons on the serious situation that confronts mankind today. As you can clearly see from Exhibits A and B, we face a mass [Exhibit A] [Exhibit B] garden hose genocide that will cripple the Yellowstone region, United States, and the world turf grass supply. According to my Nobel-overlooked masterpiece, *The Chickens Are Coming*, everyone was warned of this travesty long ago, and in that work I proposed a 650-point plan that might have possibly helped to hinder the inevitable future. The sickening feathered fowl are not the cute minuscule fluffballs they seem. Not at all. They are actually intradimensional shapeshifting Sasquatch who prefer to transmute into adorable infant hens because it gives them concealment while they obliterate their prey. Chickens are never what they appear. Admitting to their true nature would unequivocally and happily bring their reign of terror to an end.

As an illustration, I call your attention to Exhibit B. While the poultry looks innocent, a keen, trained, and brilliant mind can see the spear-point precision that the Yeti uses to penetrate the hose. Sickening, to say the least. Water wastefully washing away while we clearly see brown spots on the lawn. Because of pictures like this I have partnered with the American Turf Grass Society and Hosemakers Local 791 to develop a hardier, nearly Sasquatch-proof hose. Available at True Value for $189.95. Pertaining to the *Why* of this atrocity, I offer an explanation in my book on page 869— which can be purchased online. Frankly it is the only true explanation of this disgusting picture, although other false accounts and fairy tales do exist.

In the final analysis of the Bigfoot problem, I bring you this final, somewhat blurred, photo of the evil doppelgänger rooster fleeing into the mountains. As you have [Exhibit C] now most assuredly ordered my book, which is available online, you will know that the Bigfoot must be completely out of sight before it can change shape and slip into its extraplanar home. Thankfully after seeing these pictures, President Trump has agreed to my 650-point plan for peace. All chickens shall be immediately deported. Sasquatch must never be allowed to prey on another garden hose!"

"Well said, Doctor Chickenspear."

"Well, Craig, you must always remember: I told you so!"

Jordan Bruce
#810: An Essay

If you wipe out, you get back up and get back in the saddle. So let me tell you sumthing about wiping out—it hurts, bad. Not only physical but mental, sumtimes spiritual—all depends on how hard you slam. Slammin's all part of the game. You get knocked down, you get back up, unless you're riding stuff out like Morgan was, forget about it.

It's all about pinning it to win it, but for me I'm still down in prison, no busting laps wide open this winter. Only gym time—gotta get up! Gotta stay up and keep digging.

Now I've been lined up and competed with guys from X-Games, guys that competed with Tucker Hibbert, fastest guy alive on a sled. I'm coming for you #68. Promise. So don't slow down. Better grab another gear cuz I have no fear and I don't break check corners. I rail them so if you're railing like the T-train usually does, have fun catching my lines WFO.

That being said, I'd like to thank you for risking your life year after year. Since I was a child I've watched you race in Gaylord versus Blair Morgan #7C, and remember telling my dad I was gonna be here one day.

I made it there, to be landed on by #787 Scott Rosebush and that's why I haven't been able to catch you yet, but I'm coming—off the drugs and I'm getting my mind frame back while getting physically healthy. I don't back up and I don't back down. I'm a Yooper.

Edward Ellis Jr.
Night

Midsummer. Doomsday. I'm strolling down Van Dyke, minding my own beeswax, when suddenly I spot the grim reaper standing in the doorway of an abandoned building, his head and face shrouded beneath a billowy black cowl. Scared shitless I take off—dodging cars, bowling down pedestrians, tripping repeatedly over my own feet. Several blocks away I stop to rest, but just as I catch my breath, like the legendary phoenix, he rises from the rotting remains of a dead rat.

Heart racing, I bolt in the opposite direction. I run three, four, five miles—clear across town, only to find that he's already there, scythe in hand, waiting for me. Turn a corner, there he is. Open a door, there he is. Behind every tree, around every bend, there he is, avatar of doom, his bated breath visible even in this sweltering heat. Realizing that resistance is futile, that there's no escape, I give up the ghost. Locked in his embrace I look up into his face. It's me!

Though dead I still possess all my faculties—vision, hearing, cognition. Following a cursory check of my vitals I'm tagged, bagged, and carted off to the basement of a large, non-descript building. Like discarded dolls, dead bodies are everywhere—stacked up on tables, slumped against the walls, hanging upside down from the ceiling like butchered beef. Still warm, I'm dumped onto a cold, hard slab and stripped naked. Performing the autopsy is a little old Asian man and his two assistants, guy and a girl. "I'll be damned," the guy remarks.

"What is it?"

"I know this dude."

"Really?"

"Stayed on Van Dyke. We used to ball together. Straight up square, didn't drink, smoke, cuss, nothing. He didn't even chew gum. Paperboy, choirboy, mama's boy. Real Goody Two-Shoes."

"I hate people like that."

"Yeah, me too. I don't see any wounds on him. No cuts, no bullet holes, nothing. How'd he die?"

"Says here heart attack."

"Heart attack? He was only 19."

"Something scared him, something he saw."

"Something like what?"

"I don't know. But whatever it was, it scared him to death."

This keen assessment comes from Lola—short, pretty, thick as a brick. Built like the number eight, yet another painful reminder that crime doesn't pay. Unable to move, I wince inwardly as she shoves a catheter deep into my groin. Seconds later I feel the blood draining from my veins and listen in despair as the last few drops dribble into a rusty bucket.

"Open the chest."

Without hesitation he places a large chisel in the center of my chest and raises his mallet. I flail my arms but they don't move. I scream but to no avail. Wham! Wham! Wham! With each crushing blow the chisel sinks deeper into my sternum, and despite being dead I feel each one. Afterwards he spreads my ribs, inserts his hand into my chest cavity and carefully removes my heart.

"Excellent. We'll get top dollar for his one."

Top dollar? What the...? Wait a minute, this ain't no autopsy, and these aren't professionals. They're harvesters, bodysnatchers. They're stealing my organs! Help!! Help!! One after the other they disconnect and remove my lungs, liver and kidneys. They take my pancreas, eyes, spleen; veins, arteries, stomach. They even take my penis. "Won't be needing this no more," Lola laughs. From somewhere behind me I hear the high-pitched whine of a rotary saw followed by the sickening screech of a dull blade slicing into my cranium. With a twist and a tug he peels my scalp and scoops out my brain.

"All right, that's a wrap, nice work. Run these over to Doc, he's waiting for 'em. Who we got next?"

"Black male, 15, multiple gunshots."

"Drug dealer, gangbanger?"

"Honor student. Cops killed him."

"God bless America. We ready? Okay, get him in here before he spoils. Let's go, chop chop!"

Stripped like a stolen Escalade, I lay down on that cold, hard, bloody slab shivering like a shorn sled dog. For a long as I can remember I've had the vague but unmistakable feeling that I was being watched, followed, stalked. I could feel it in my bones, the muffled footsteps of something trying to sneak up on me. I'd turn around but there'd be nothing there, just the lingering impression that fate was slowly gaining on me, little by little, moving in for the kill. Every hour, every episode, had nudged me closer to this, my destiny, until now, at the tender age of 19, suddenly I find myself standing on the precipice of doom, starting into the abyss, with no way out.

Feech
Untitled

The penal institution, oubliette, reformatory, the big house, gaol, the joint. All these designations are used to describe one place: prison. Commonly defined as a place of confinement where people are kept while waiting for trial or while serving time for breaking the law. Some might call it a place where you "find yourself," maybe discover religion or possibly find your purpose—that meaning in life. Countless have agreed that having gone to prison struck a time in their lives where all that was assimilated was lost.

When hearing the phrase "you have been sentenced to 'x' amount of time in prison," what does that do to a man or woman emotionally? A feeling of trepidation, abatement, anguish or for some, instant remorse for their victim or crime. Sadly, for those who are locked up in the U.S. and abroad who break laws governed to protect the people, they aren't always placed in facilities that cater to their crime. For example: a first-time offender or person of low risk could be and most likely is placed into an amalgam with different levels of felons—arsonists, rapists, and murderers. In retrospect, that person should be placed in a facility with those of the same level of crime or combination. For instance, why are there more and more new cases of those with diagnosed mental disabilities entering the prison system? Shouldn't we be trying to succor them the way they need to be? Wouldn't that make us stronger as a society, a country, and as human beings?

Correctional institutions are portrayed as the type of place a person goes to help "correct" their behaviors or wrongdoings, yet most are becoming training grounds for learning to become better criminals. Of course this statement is mainly geared toward those not wanting help or to acquire new positive knowledge from the experience of being locked up. I do believe one's location and the people he or she is surrounded by have a deep impact on the way they perceive life situations, view themselves, function inside prison and later on the outside and knowing there are ways to properly deal with future problems.

While many use the time to reflect, meditate, and self-rehabilitate through reading and taking advantage of educational opportunities offered to do what they need to acclimate themselves back into society, by "law" a public file of the individual's mistake(s)—(a.k.a. crimes)—is sometimes broadcasted and made easy for the public (i.e., potential employers, family, colleges, etc.) to access. What do most do when they come across someone's criminal record, look past it and think nothing of it? Unfortunately, the majority has a preconceived notion of that person and their character maybe even before meeting. Ask yourself this

question: why have an out date or see a parole board to "judge" if ʼ
to go back into society, if "society" has already written you off? "He oɪ ˍ
is a criminal, we can't hire them" or "they aren't to be trusted because they
were locked up at a point." A lot of jobs parolees or ex-cons are applying
for have little or nothing to do with their initial crime(s). Do you think
these individuals are hired or given a fair opportunity? What does that say
about the hiring process, discrimination and the way people look down
on those with a record? This message is in no way to put anyone in the
mindset of "don't try, give up or go out and re-offend because there is no
future." There is a future and a bright one for those willing to change their
lifestyle and way of thinking. This message is to educate those who know:
1. how hard it is to find employment without a record, and 2. to show that
all who are LABELED (and yes, that's all it is, is a LABEL) as criminals
aren't inferior, dangerous and unproductive members of society. Certain
choices led to negative outcomes in a lot of our lives and for the most part
many are seeking forgiveness and a chance for redemption.

Take for example guys who have been "down" for 10 years, 20 years
or more. They will tell you, "this isn't the place to be" or "there's time to
still change yourself." They themselves have been in and out of the system
and experienced loss, years that can't be replaced. Some guys know what
it's like to wake up in a Level IV or V each morning and have to grab a
weapon to defend themselves for the day; what it's like to not see, to hear
from or to have loved ones pass while being incarcerated—or to get paid
$.84 for a full day's work. And, for the select few, live day in and day out
knowing that ERD (Earliest Release Date) or RD (Release Date) is non-
existent. Is this the life I want or plan to continue leading?... No!

Now, I can't speak for everyone and as mad as it sounds, some
enjoy being locked up. For a lot of those who have little on the outside,
no family/support system—jail/prison provides a home and all the
necessities one needs to survive. Free housing, no bills, free medical,
dental for a small fee, and three meals a day. From what I understand
from a lot of the old school guys who have been "down" since the early
70s, the food and pay was spot-on in their time. Minimum wage jobs
were being offered throughout the compound. The food was "real" and
in larger portions. A lot of the meals we receive now are processed;
"nutritionist recommended," right. Most guys refer to the meat as "cat
head" purely because the size is close in comparison.

All this to say: are laws meant and written to continuously punish
and bind those who have already paid their debt to society? To hang over
one's head like a dark cloud for the rest of one's life and not mitigate us to
become stronger people? When someone is judged on a crime years in
the past with no current convictions—how does that help that individual

to mentally overcome and rebuild themselves? It almost lowers a man or woman's self-worth in a sense.

Through my short stint of being incarcerated, I'll be using current and life lessons to make it through, overcoming the obstacles society and the laws put on myself and others as convicts and ex-convicts. The only way to do that is in all but one word: faith.

John C. Gaik IV
My Uncle Wrestled Sharks

My uncle wrestled sharks. He wrestled them all of the time, from the Baja Peninsula to the Bahamas. He once told us that you have to wrestle a shark in chest-deep water. "You gotta even the playing field," he said. "What do you think, that I'm loco, that I wrestle them in the deep? No, there's no leverage."

My uncle was the only adult at our family's big Fourth of July get-together who drank out of a long can. He took a hearty swallow and set the can down in the grass next to his thick, bare feet where he sat. "You go chest deep!" he said, humorously beating his soft chest with two quick slaps, cementing the moment solidly into my memory forever. "First you gotta fish them in from the shore, just for sport. Then you gotta wrestle them for ART. That's the poetry in motion, little *sobrinos*."

A few months later he missed my eighth birthday. As it turned out, he had gotten into the fight of his life with a mako in Sydney, Australia. This was farther than he had ever traveled. It was important, he explained, that the sharks knew who he was down there too. He called from "the land down under" to tell my brothers and I all about what he referred to as the Battle in the Reefs.

That year I had a brand new bicycle sitting in the living room. It was my first mountain bike, a ten speed, and I didn't even take it out until the next day. I was too young to understand that my father had worked hard to buy me that bicycle for my birthday, with money we couldn't afford to spend. He was reluctant to put my uncle on speaker phone, but my brothers and I begged and pleaded.

We went wild, jumping on the bed and rolling into each other, when he said he had to finally jam his fingers, knuckle deep, into the shark's nostrils. He did this for control, of course. Then he acted like it was no big deal. There was a temporary silence on the phone. We crowded in closer, shushing one another, as we waited to hear of what our courageous uncle had done next. I glanced over to my dad, who stood quietly in the corner with his arms crossed. He looked up and forced a closed-mouth smile for me on my birthday.

"It was just a baby mako," my uncle continued, "only seven feet. I wore it down enough to get some teeth, though." That's what he would always tell us, because you see, that's when it was really beat. When he could pull out his special pliers and extract a few teeth for us, that was a successful wrestling match. We exploded in cheer for his victory.

Shark teeth cost next to nothing at hokey little shops, but these were different. The ones in my collection were priceless, ripped from the mouths of sharks that my uncle had wrestled in my honor. *Lo hizo en mi honor.* Eight teeth came in the mail with a birthday card five weeks later.

On Christmas Eve my uncle wasn't feeling well after he fell on the back porch at my grandmother's house. He was taken to one of the bedrooms by the men of our family. There was an argument over him. He was later helped outside to the backseat of the car to take him home. We chased after him with our hands out, and although he was very sick, our hands soon became filled with a multitude of various shark teeth that he gave us from his pockets.

With each tooth, I imagined a different wrestling match. With each tooth, we created different stories as to how they came to be in my uncle's possession. We traded our stories like old Indian mystics with the addition of my uncle's gusto. I didn't know it then, but this was the day I became a writer, though I believe I was learning all along.

The winter and spring had come and gone without a word from our uncle. He did not appear at any of the family gatherings. We had come to rely on his stories. So as each of my brothers' and cousins' birthdays passed by without the phone ringing, we continued to imagine one epic scenario after another. He would come back, we told ourselves. He had to come back. We understood what he was doing. After all, the world was a big place, and my uncle had a lot of coastline to conquer. He would have more to tell than ever before. That was the way we looked at it.

Then the dreams started. Anybody who says people don't dream in color is wrong. The exotic images of my uncle with the sharks were some of the most pleasant I've ever seen. Some of them horrified me, though, and woke me out of my sleep. With these dreams came the visions of death struggles between my uncle and the emotionless creatures. He would come up out of the ocean at dusk, breaking the surface with a great white thrashing in his arms. Then they would slam sideways back into the water together with a hard smack! They would do this repeatedly, for what seemed like all night, as I slept. They would rise up, his wrists locked around the shark's waist, his chin buried into the slick gray skin of its back. He hit the water hard and grew weaker each time. The shark was too strong. I felt what he felt, the loss of leverage as he took the water in through his mouth and nose.

I would sit up in the darkness trying to catch my breath for a moment as my brothers snoozed all around me, consumed by their own dreams. I would quietly pull out my box of shark teeth, examine them under the moonlight coming in through my window, and feel comfort in knowing that no shark could beat my uncle. Another year passed like this.

July Fourth arrived again, and this time, so did my uncle. He pulled up into the driveway on a little old motorcycle, and we all ran out to meet him. He wore a leather jacket even though it was 85 degrees. He was somehow shorter and little fatter, and he wore black boots and oversized sunglasses, but to us he was the coolest thing we had ever seen. He was silent as he got down from the bike and stood it up. There were at least a dozen of us boys, my brothers and all of my cousins, surrounded around him. Then he took the big, rose tinted glasses off, held out his arms, and yelled, "¡Mi sobrinos!" and the wall that had been built up by nearly two years of his absence had disintegrated at once. This was how strong he was.

We all screamed, pawing at him and hugging him. Like a mob through the streets of jubilee, we followed him through to the back yard where he greeted everybody. Some of them didn't have very much to say, so he nodded and kept walking. He constantly ruffled our hair and made us laugh. The kids were easy to please.

He filled up a plate at the long table of food. "The trick is to always load your plate with everything, and always make it look like you emptied your plate. It makes every lady in our family happy." Then he whispered out of the side of his mouth some advice just for me, "And hey kiddo, if you don't like it, feed it to one of your grandma's dogs. Unless it's your Aunt Rosie's cooking, they won't eat it."

My uncle was the only adult at our family's big Fourth of July get-together who poured liquid from a flat bottle in his pocket into a soda pop can. "Where were you? Where did you go?" we begged of him as he drank and licked barbecue sauce off his fingers.

He leaned forward. "I'll tell you where I was. I was everywhere— Brazil, Ireland, South Africa, and even Japan—just to name a few. A tribe of cannibals tried to eat me in Papua New Guinea, kept me captive in a little hut. They were gonna roast me like a pig, but they let me go when I showed them how to take care of their tiger shark problem. I was out to the Hawaiian Islands too. There I wrestled the greatest killer of them all, the great white."

I was shocked. Were my dreams real, I wondered?

"I've been building up to this one for some time now—training my muscles, my mind, my heart." He gestured to each as he said them. "That's why I've been gone so long." He slowly crossed his eyes in solemn recognition of those memories. We were all deeply impressed. "It was a long battle, a match I thought would never end. I outlasted him, though, and finally did him in with a full nelson. His fins will be so sore he won't swim straight for a week."

He took another drink and a few more bites from his plate. Then he suddenly winced, killing the vibe at once. "Yikes! I can handle a great white shark, but I still can't handle your Aunt Rosie's cooking. I should have been training for that." We exploded with laughter. "Hey, where are those ugly little dogs your *abuela* keeps around?" We all laughed together, and he winked at me.

My birthday arrived. I blew out ten candles, made one wish, and like a miracle it came true. My father's cell phone suddenly rang, and without his permission I ran and picked it up. I was surprised to hear a robotic voice. "This is a call from a correctional facility and is subject to monitoring and recording. Thank you for using TeleLink."

"Hey, where's my little nephew at?" came my uncle's enthusiastic voice. "I have to make this one quick. I don't have a lot of money on the account."

"No uncle, it's me!" I shrieked.

There was a long silence. Then he burst through the line as if he were right there in front of me. "This morning, guess where I was, nephew?"

I listened to the story without a word. His voice faded as I began to grow numb. The more I thought about it, the more I began to know the truth. A correctional facility? That's jail.

As it turned out, my uncle had never even set foot on a beach or seen the ocean in his entire life. My uncle had a lot of problems and missed a lot of birthdays. My uncle wrestled with demons. Though he called them something else. My uncle wrestled sharks.

Maine Harrell
Heavy is the Womb That Bears Black Boys

Heavy is the womb that bears black boys. It is, after all, the mother lode. Crucible to men and mankind alike. Humanity drew its breath there and civilization found its origins. Our mothers have given the world rulers, revolutionaries, scholars, and soldiers. Black mothers have given the world life.

In Amerika hardship and struggle have been their recompense. Here, our mothers saw themselves pimped in service of chattel slavery, their wombs opened for the business of brutality. Their children were born to serve, to be sold or, if not, to be slain. Still they endured.

They held families together with determination, courage, and grit. They survived labor pains and the pains of slavery's labors. For freedom they fought, killed, and died. And as always, black mothers kept right on giving life.

Today the struggles continue, and thus, so do the triumphs. Our mothers rear genius in an Amerika that scoffs at black intellect. They conjure pride in children ashamed of simply being and, in their hands, minimum-wage jobs become like lead to an alchemist.

As always, death shadows them, their seed. They used to see their boys auctioned off to unknown plantations; now they weep as damn near a generation of us are carted away to maximum-security nether worlds. They used to see us lynched; now they cradle our corpses in blood soaked streets.

Through it all their love remains transcendent, unconditional. They love us when we're right, when we're wrong. They love us in spite of all we think we are, all we'll ever—and never—be. No doubt, some of our mothers fear us for reasons real and imagined, but they embrace us nevertheless. We're still their sons.

And just as their sons have been demonized, so have they. The black mother has been reincarnated as the worst sort of social parasite, from crack ho to welfare queen. She's the bug-eyed bullying matriarch on that "new sitcom," the cold-hearted careerist bitch on the talk shows. Still, mama endures.

Which isn't to suggest our mothers are perfect, they aren't. Sometimes their pressures—sexism, racism, mounting debts, fears that one day Junior might not make it home—become too intense, too heavy. Sometimes they're just not prepared for the obligations of motherhood. Sometimes fissures riddle their armor and they go under, to drugs or to liquor or to a wholesale psychological shutdown.

They hurt us, they use us, they leave us.

Who in Amerika, however, can stand in judgment of black mothers? Who can really know their burden, their pains? Who can really know the fears and expectations and hopes of women whose sons, it often seems, are born only to die! Black men may love our mothers, cherish and respect them. We may be as familiar with them as well as anyone. But who, besides our mothers themselves, truly understands how heavy is the womb that bears black boys?

D.L. Hemphill
Another Day in Prison

A buzzing sound wakes me. I open my eyes to find it's the blinding fluorescent light beaming down on me. Another day in prison begins. I drape my legs off the side of the top bunk, careful not to kick my cellmate sleeping three feet below me.

Like a gymnast, I dismount from the top bunk onto a rickety plastic stool. My feet just miss dead center and the stool shoots out from beneath me. I crash to the floor but my thud vanishes in the bang of the stool bouncing off the steel door.

My cellmate rolls over and sneers at me.

"Sorry about that, bunkie," I say as I lurch to my feet.

He just shakes his head, hisses out a breath, and rolls back over.

I rub my elbow. The sharp pain distracts me from my kinked neck and sore back. Damn that two-inch thick green thing that the state has nerve to call a mattress! I could really use some aspirin. If I put them on my store list today, I'll have them in just two weeks.

My cellmate is already beginning to snore again. I hate to make more noise but I really have to pee. With my back facing him, I squeeze myself between his bunk and the toilet. The sound or urine hitting water sounds like Niagara Falls in our broom closet-sized room. But I feel relieved and I relax a bit. MISTAKE! A pent up fart escapes, clouding my cellmate's head. The smell wakes him, and he roughly pulls his blanket over his head. I'm sure later on the yard he will be complaining about me to anyone who will listen.

I look at my plastic Casio watch. It's already 6:10. That leaves me about enough time before they call breakfast for a bitter cup of instant coffee and a teeth brushing. Unfortunately, this requires the use of our unusually loud sink. I turn it on and wince as the pipes sputter and shake.

Quickly I notice that the water spewing out is almost as dark as the coffee I'm trying to make. This happens whenever the wind blows hard enough to shake the rust-filled tower. I wish I had a few spoons of sugar to mask the chemical taste but the administration recently restricted it, supposedly to stop prisoners from making wine. Thinking back these past 10 years I can rarely recall ever even seeing wine. But everybody knows administration uses any excuse to take things from us. I pull to memory all the other things they have taken away, counting off each one on my fingers: cigarettes, razors, typewriters, soda, toasters, duffel bags, hot plates and visiting outfits, to just name a few.

I'm barely finished brushing my teeth in rust colored water when I hear people walking past my door. I lean out and give my neighbor a questioning look.

"Breakfast," he informs me.

I tense up. The officers purposely whisper the mealtime calls. But stop for two seconds at someone's cell and the walls rumble with their screams.

I slide out into the hall, locking the door behind me. Some people leave theirs open, but I trust no one. The walk to the chow hall is quiet. Most of the inmates are still in their own medicated zombie-like states from the boatload of Seroquel that medical shoves down their throats. I'm not worried though, they'll stop giving it out when the pharmaceutical kickbacks to the medical department dry up.

The line for breakfast stretches out the chow hall doors. The guy behind me is standing so close that I can feel his rancid breath warm the back of my neck. I turn around to yell at him but I stop when I see he's an old man. What would be the point? If the guy hasn't learned manners by now then nothing I say will change him. I turn back around and see the line hasn't moved an inch. How is this even possible? Then I see. Like VIPs at a nightclub, people that think they're special cut straight to the front of the line.

A half hour later, I'm handed a tray of runny oatmeal.

"Where's the waffles?" I ask.

"We're out," the food steward curtly replies.

I go to the next empty seat but skip it when I notice someone had spilled orange juice all over it.

"Inmate!" a voice shouts.

I turn to an officer glaring at me.

"Fill in that seat," he instructs me, pointing to the juice covered chair.

"There's juice on it," I argue.

"Use your napkin."

I know this is not an argument I can win with logic so I comply and use my only napkin to smear around the mess. At this point, I lost my appetite. When I get up to leave, I can feel my damp pants sticking to the seat.

I get back to my cell and notice the trash bin is out in front of my door. This is the universal prison code for I'm using the bathroom. I look at my watch. It's only 6:50, and the unit won't open for movement until 7 o'clock. I scratch my chin and wonder if my cellmate is really using the bathroom, or if this is payback for waking him up this morning. Either way if I get caught standing here and officer will write me a ticket. I slide into the water closet and hide for the next 10 minutes.

The dayroom opens and I sit in there for the next hour while I wait on staff to call big yard. The television is blaring, but I'm still unable to hear it over everyone's shouts and screams. Finally I hear an officer over the intercom.

"Big yard," he shouts into the mic.

I get up to leave, but I'm stopped in my tracks when he adds, "Is cancelled."

My shoulders sink and I let out a groan. That's the third time this week. There's a hundred officers working, and if one decides to leave early, they claim there isn't enough officers to open the yard. I shuffle my feet out of the building and go to the tiny dirty lot they call our small yard. The dirt track is turned to mud from last night's rain. I'm the only one out there so maybe I can get a little exercise in. After some minor stretching, I start to slowly jog. If I go any faster around the small hundred-foot track I might get dizzy, but I never get the chance.

"Hey you!" a passing officer yells. "There's no running on the small yard."

I look at him like he's crazy, "Why?"

"Because of the risk of you crashing into someone and hurting them."

I look around the empty yard. "I'm the only one out here."

His lips pinch together and his cheeks redden. "I'm not going to argue with you, run again and you'll be in the hole."

I throw my hands up in surrender then stomp off, back to my cell. I guess I'll knock out my shaving, then shower. I pull out my electric razor and get half of my head shaved when the batteries die. I go to my footlocker for some more only to find that the dead ones were my last two. I appraise the damage in the mirror. If I stand to one side, I have hair, and if I turn to the other side, I'm bald. "Damn them for taking the razors," I mutter under my breath.

Soap and towel in hand I head for the shower. "Yes!" I say pumping my fist into the air. For once, there's no line. I have the entire shower to myself. After getting undressed, I hang my clothes on the hooks and turn the corner into the shower. "You gotta be kidding me!" my scream echoes. There, in the center of the shower floor, is a steaming pile of human crap. I can hear giggles coming from the hallway, but I don't see the humor in this.

Naked already I decide to shower anyways. Like a game of twister, I manage to carefully sidestep the human feces that's liquefying past my feet on its way to the drain.

Dried and dressed I go downstairs to pick up my clean clothing from the unit laundry man. He hands me my bag of whites back, and the pit of my stomach falls. Everything's stained a deep copper like orange. I slap my hand against my forehead. The rusty water got me again.

I go back to my cell and fold them. They confiscated my duffle bag so I have to cram them into my locker.

I check my watch and see that it's almost count time. I climb onto my bunk and settle in for the next hour and a half. The mailroom has denied the last three books I ordered, so I'm forced to grab one of the books that I have already read. Threat to the security of the institution, they say. How they can find Harry Potter a threat I'll never know.

It's noon now, and I'm glad to be able to leave my cell. The dayroom is shoulder-to-shoulder standing room only because everyone wants to be first out the doors for lunch. We get the call, and like a herd of sheep, we walk to the chow hall.

The line is even longer and slower since everyone is awake by lunch. The menu reads spaghetti and meat sauce, but they give me over cooked noodles with a dollop of ketchup. I'm starving, so I scarf it down before I can even taste it.

Leaving the chow hall, I notice the officers haven't even called the next unit. I let out a bitter laugh and shake my head. These officers purposely hold the lines up until 1:45, shift change. That way they don't have to run big yard until 2:30, effectively robbing us of an hour of yard.

At 2:30, the yard reopens. I want to go outside, but I know this will be the only hour today that my cellmate will be gone. Sitting down at the desk, I begin to write to the girl that I thought I would spend the rest of my life with. She hasn't answered any of my recent phone calls. I think that she has found someone else.

I'm disrupted by a rapping on my door. I look up and see an officer. I open the door knowing this can't be good.

"Step out so I can shake your cell down," he says in an emotionless tone.

He doesn't even let me slip on my shoes. Walking down to the end of the hall the smacking of my flip-flops against the grimy concrete alerts my neighbors to the possibility that they may be next.

A half hour later, the officer exits my cell. He's carrying two pieces of cardboard that doubled as makeshift shelves inside my locker.

"Fire hazard," he says, obviously reading the look of confusion painted across my face.

I give him the palms up gesture. "Fire hazard? So you are telling me that the locker that I'm assigned to keep all of my highly flammable prison clothes in can't have a piece of cardboard in it because it's flammable?"

The officer aggressively leans towards me and raises his voice. "If you want to argue about it, then I'll just write you a ticket right now."

I can tell he's trying to get a rise out of me, so I decide to keep my mouth shut. He takes it as a victory and struts off.

I go back to my cell to check the damage. I'm at a loss for words. I have to take a step back and collect myself. It looks like the cell was hit by a hurricane, during a robbery. Mattresses flipped, food stomped on, clothes in the toilet, coffee spilled, and everything of mine is mixed with my cellmate's.

I spend the remainder of my alone time separating our things. When my cellmate comes back, he's even madder than I am. Great, I think to myself. Now I've got to listen to him complain for the next hour and a half.

I hop onto my bunk and attempt to sleep away the time. Unfortunately, the scorching afternoon sun has made it to our side of the building. The rays heat up the bricks and shoot through the windows, turning the room into an oven. I'm having trouble breathing. I continuously sip on the rusty water to replenish the sweat that is soaking through my clothes. The next 90 minutes feel like an eternity.

Five o'clock finally arrives, and I peel myself from the mat and race down to the dayroom, hoping to get a spot in front of the big fan. I don't even come close. I find a spot on a corner table in the back. I really want to rest my head on the cool stainless steel, but the risk of catching the flesh-eating disease that's been going around makes me think better of it.

A while later, they call for dinner. Meatballs, they say. A starving dog would turn up his nose at this meal. I'll go just to get the milk and the fruit.

At the end of the line, I see the food steward. She could possibly pass for cute if she would stop giving such dirty looks to all the inmates. I scratch my head. Her attitude seems weird in contrast to the affection she shows towards the male officers.

I shrug it off and go to my table. I can feel the chill of the milk through the thin cardboard box. I take a huge gulp and already have it swallowed before the sourness hits my taste buds. "Yuck, the milk's spoiled." I announce to no one in particular. Everyone begins sniffing their milk like glasses of fine wine.

Me, I had enough. Pocketing my apple for later, I dump my tray and leave the chow hall.

Halfway down the sidewalk an officer stops me.

"What's in your pocket?" he asks pointing at the round bulge protruding from my thigh.

I shrug and pull out the apple.

He smiles, takes the apple, and pitches it in the garbage with the rest of the food that he had confiscated.

I glare at him until he tells me to "push on."

Back in the unit I sit on the desk in my cell and stare at the cinderblock wall. This gets real boring real fast, so I walk down to the dayroom. The second I get down there, I feel out of place. How can I be surrounded by so many people and still feel alone? I spend the next two hours walking meaninglessly between my cell and dayroom, occasionally making small talk with people whose names I can't remember.

Eight o'clock rolls by. I dress down into a pair of shorts and climb back up on my bunk. I lie back on my thin mat and prop my head up on a folded pillow so I can see the television at the end of my bunk. There's no remote so I stretch my left out and use my big toe to flick through the stations. I've been changing stations like this for so long that my right calf is now noticeably bigger than my left one.

After a couple more hours of this, I turn the television off and get ready for bed.

Crawling between my rust-stained sheets, I close my eyes and try to fall asleep before the officer shines his light in my face on his next round.

Lying there in the darkness, I replay the day's events in my head. I've made it through another day in prison. Just 7000 more to go and then I'll be home. I just hope that they all can be as good as today was.

Corey Joseph Montague
When Detroit Had Had the Superbad!

In the 70s, 80s, and 90s. When Detroit had the World Boxing Association (WBA) on LOCKDOWN! We had profoundly talented prize fighters at Kronk's Gym like Steve McCrory, Donald Curry, Caveman Lee, Ricky Womack, Kevin Whaley—Qué El—and Thomas "Hitman" Hearns, just to name a few. Detroit had some super Baddddd Boys! But the game would be remiss if it didn't at least pay homage to a local fallen star. One whose light shined brightly, but ever so briefly. Minus the glitz and glamour of this boxer's alcoholic life. This is the sad but very true story of Arthur Bernard "Superbad" Mays, 1960-1994.

Superbad was born to Victoria Mays and Prince Milton. In the late 70s, Warren Avenue was the boulevard of inquities. As a teen on the Numbers Streets of Detroit's Southwest side, he survived off government cheese, low poverty, and high crime. Replete with gang violence, drug-infested neighborhoods, pimps, whores slamming Cadillac doors, stuck-up kids and con artists selling slim jewelry. The black culture is still used to phases like "Gimme some skin" or "Gimme five on the black hand side," "Jive turkey," and "Sho' you right!" Where the latest styles were Afro hairdos, bell-bottom pants, and platform shoes, and screaming, "Black Power!"

A pubescent Bernard and his friends Eric Williams and Collier Blunt would skip school to stand in front of a liquor store, panhandling customers for loose change while catcalling at neighborhood young girls on their way to school. The boys drank malt liquor beer and Wild Irish Rose wine. They'd drunkenly sing on the side of the liquor store in an awkward attempt at harmonization, totally butchering the Temptations' "My Girl." Eric Williams recalled, "Bernard and I had been drinking and smoking since we were 14."

The super-bad pugilist, a young man who could've been a contender, missed his shot at a successful future. From the doorsteps of life, he battled his greatest foe of them all deep within himself: his alcoholism. Mays took to the sweet science like a shark took to two rows of razor sharp teeth! He has cold-blooded timing with knockout power in both fists inside the ring. Superbad was as elusive as a shadow and quicker than a scalded dog.

"Speed is power" so sayeth John John about Mays, "The punch you can't see is the one that knocks your ass out!"

Superbad danced, flicking wicked pistol-shot jabs, bobbing and weaving, slipping punches, throwing uppercuts, combinations, left or right hooks, and overhand rights with the impact of plastic explosives.

At home, Bernard didn't get along well with his alcoholic father, Prince Milton. So in between bouts with him, Bernard bounced around Detroit's west side living off and on with his childhood friend, Collier Blunt, who was also a talented boxer like Bernard. Collier's beloved mother, Mrs. Lucille Blunt, loved Bernard like a son. She'd welcome him into her Ohio Street home off Grand River. Many nights, he'd crash on her couch, snoring off drunkenness, only to awaken to a serious hangover and hot breakfast served with a smile. However, back at the Mays homestead, testosterone levels between father and son ran high. At 14, Prince Milton abandoned Bernard's mother and sister, Esther. One day, Bernard's second cousin, Charles "Big Tuna" Jordan, a journeyman heavyweight fighter, suggested, "Bernard, you be on the streets fightin' and knockin' dudes our fo' free. Why not learn how to get paid fo' yo' knuckle game?"

Big Tuna introduced Bernard to International Boxing Hall of Fame inductee and legendary trainer Emanuel Steward. Steward was the mastermind of 50 amateur champions and Olympic Gold medalists. He won 40 World Championships, 120 titles, and more than $150 million in purse monies at Kronk Boxers Club. When Steward saw Mays spar, needless to say he was impressed. Soon Bernard earned the moniker, Superbad.

Emanuel Steward says, "Superbad won 200 straight amatuer bouts, lost only one amatuer fight and one pro fight."

While sparring with him, Thomas "Hitman" Hearns complained about Bernard Mays. "I could smell liquor on his breath. Hell, when we sparred, he was usually drunk most of the time off Colt .45 malt liquor. But the boy was baddd. No… I meant Superbad!" Hearns continued, "He almost made me quit fighting. Cuz, when I went to the gym, I knew Emanuel would pair us. I knew it was always gonna be ah' battle."

Bernard was cursed with a genetic predisposition to alcohol. He couldn't control his urges. Drinking was his form of spiritual escape. Briefly, alcohol had the opposite effect on him, whereas other alcoholics couldn't function intoxicated. Bernard became aggressive and physically excelled. His reflexes seemed to become enhanced. He'd carouse and do a 24 close bars and then hit the after-hours joints with older ladies. He'd dance all night like Fred Astaire and spend money on the ladies like a millionaire. He loved older, more seasoned women. Psychologists called his erogenous stimulation an Oedipus complex. Women his own age gave him heartburn. After an all-nighter of hard core drinking and toxic sex, he'd pop up in the gym and beat sparks off the asses of anyone Emanuel placed in the ring.

In 1977, Jimmy Paul, former lightweight champ, intimated, "That guy was at the National Ohio State Fair Tournament. Bernard would be out with the ladies drinking all night long, then come into the ring and totally destroy his opponents." Also in '77, Bernard went across the pond to London, England. Not only had he beaten the European amateur champion, but he had also knocked his ass out cold! Bernard was a tournament winner at 14 and 106 pounds, and in the National Junior Olympic Tournament, he won again in the 130-pound division. He was the greatest fighter there ever was. He was like Sugar Ray Robinson—he had it all. Emanuel noted, "He started disappearing before workouts. Personally aloof, he'd get moody and stop coming to the gym regularly. By 16, he was an alcoholic off Colt .45."

In 1978, disgruntled with Emanuel Steward, Mays hired prominent attorney, Elbert Hatchett. Bernard soon left Steward. Superbad turned pro under Chuck Davis. Davis, a disciple of Emanuel Steward, was an international drug smuggler. He shipped drugs across the pond using Bernard and other fighters as unwitting drug mules. He was later indicted by the FBI. Davis had a gym in the Herman Gardens Projects. Bernard trained there and signed his first contract, receiving a whopping $100 for his first fight at Northwest Activity Center. The house was packed.

In 1979, he fought at Cobo Hall and Joe Louis Arena.

[Mays v Bobby Howard]

Managers and bookmakers were seated in the first, second, and third rows. They had paid good money to see Superbad perform, and he didn't disappoint. He demolished Howard despite Chuck's gangster street credentials. When it came to taming Bernard Mays, however, Chuck had his hands full when Bernard wanted malt liquor. He usually got malt liquor. Davis would resort to some extreme measures to prevent him from drinking. Sometimes Davis locked doors and windows and physically restrained him. Rumor has it, Davis literally tied Bernard to a bed. Meanwhile, another rumor floated, that he'd handcuffed him naked to a radiator, forcing him into cold turkey withdrawal. Whatever the case, Bernard Mays was an extraordinary talent. As a pro, he'd been a winner, but in California, his winning streak came to an abrupt end, as did his spectacular career. As fate dictates to reality, a hard liver shot in the third round caused him to spit blood. When the fight was over, Bernard needed help to get out of the ring. Attorney Elbert Hatchett had him hospitalized and paid for his travel expenses home. Bernard Superbad Mays had reached his bitter endgame. For him to re-lace his gloves would mean death.

Near the end of his life, Bernard convalesced at his mother's home. He lived off of $550 Social Security a month, $200 food stamps, and

Medicare. With his mother's passing, Superbad was unable to care for himself. Heartbroken and a sickly diabetic, he was forced to move into New Light Nursing Home at Grand River and Chicago. His health continued to deteriorate. Chronic malabsorption syndrome was among his ailments. On good days, sometimes he was able to roam the nursing home hallways with his IV in tow, flirting with nurses and visitors. But on bad days, Superbad was a shell of his former self. His belly swelled to the size of a brown medicine ball, his skin became chalky, and his hair dry and lifeless. Yet his sharp mind remained alert. He knew his friends and kept them animated whenever they cared enough to visit. Bernard put on a brave face knowing he was nearing the final bell of his last round.

Bernard Superbad Mays left this world to enter eternity a contender on March 1, 1994. His remains are located at Mt. Hazel Cemetery. If you visit his gravesite, it would break any real boxing-lover's heart. He's lying in an unkempt grave—on Detroit's west side. Oh, and by the way, Bernard can be found in a sorrowfully dilapidated unmarked grave, surrounded by thick overgrowth. Section 4, row 18, grave No. 36. An ignominious fate for such a helluva pugilist. For boxing lovers around the world—we salute the Superbad!

Quentin Jones
Not How or What But Why

Every day I watch the news or read the newspaper I learn of another senseless act of violence perpetrated by one black person against another. In particular, young black males for whom the chances of becoming a victim of homicide are greater than the chances of going to college.

Every time that I hear politicians, lawmakers, or our supposed black leaders discuss this topic the focus is always on the "How?" and "What?" but never the "Why?"—as in "how can we stop black-on-black violence?" and "What," as in "what laws can one create to punish the perpetrators of these acts?" If one is really serious about addressing the issue of black-on-black violence, then it is imperative that one must start focusing on the "Why?" "Why," as in "why is black-on-black violence so prevalent in this country?" It seems that nobody ever wants to discuss the "Why?" I guess because in doing so one would undoubtedly expose the flawed system that is designed to destroy black lives, but appears to promote FREEDOM, JUSTICE, and EQUALITY.

It's not a coincidence that black-on-black violence is most prevalent in the urban communities where there is a lack of education, lack of resources, residential segregation, high unemployment rates, and poverty. These conditions play a significant role in the black-on-black violence epidemic. In addition, the average family living within the urban community is living below the poverty line. On the surface it may appear that black-on-black violence is nothing more than crimes being committed by criminals, but it is much deeper than that. The system that was supposedly designed to ensure equality to all American citizens has failed us. Yes, black people have to accept some responsibility for the black-on-black violence epidemic, but one also has to consider all other external factors which contribute to black-on-black violence.

First, let's examine the lack of education, which I consider to be the most significant external factor contributing to black-on-black violence. Why are so many schools being closed in black communities? Why do suburban schools use computers in the early years, while urban schools either don't use computers or start much later? Why is the curriculum taught at the urban schools outdated, thus putting urban students at a disadvantage academically? Why is it that the least qualified teachers go to the urban community schools while the more qualified teachers go to the suburban schools? The lack of education in black communities contributes, again, to high unemployment and poverty and thus the epidemic. Many variables exist which underscore the concept of black-on-black violence, and contrary to what contemporary America wants the public to believe, black males are not some hyper-violent, super-predatory animals, whose innate nature is to kill. Rather, black people, for innumerable years, have been and continue to be so oppressed that some of us have, ultimately, become hopeless.

I would argue that the root of black-on-black violence is internalized self-hate, which stems all the way back to the era of slavery. For over 400 years black people have endured some of the most atrocious acts of hate known to humankind at the hands of Europeans. These centuries of hatred have had a damaging, psychological effect on all black people. Therefore, black males in particular, who have long been targeted for extinction, have unconsciously developed a self-hate complex. What this means is that black males have internalized all of the hate inflicted upon one's self for centuries, and have subconsciously started to hate other black people thus perpetrating the original slavemaster's mentality. Hence the black-on-black violence epidemic plaguing this country right now. Black-on-black violence is a very serious issue—one that needs to be immediately addressed. However, the solution doesn't lie so much in the "How?" or "What?" but rather in the "Why?"

So long as there is a minimal focus on the "Why," and black people constantly lack knowledge of self, black-on-black violence will continue to run rampant within this country. But then again, maybe that's their goal.

Just a little food for thought…

Steven T. Lake
How I Learned About Passing Time

As I close in on Arizona, I am struck by the staggering realization that I have done it again. I promised myself that I wouldn't let anything come between me and the freedom I had been working so hard for these last few miserable years, the tiny crumb of the American Dream that ants like me crawl for… yet here I am, in the middle of the desert, driving into a savage sunset, with the creeping fear that they know where I am heading, and who I am heading there to kill.

I had reached the breaking point in New Orleans. I had known I was close to crossing the fuck-it line just as soon as I got off the Greyhound bus and saw the look in her eyes. The look said, "I really don't want to be here, and I really don't want *you* to be here."

I had called her from the bus the night before, using a phone I borrowed from my seatmate Jimmy, a fairly laid-back fellow that looked to be in his early 30s, whom I met when I first got on the bus in Michigan. He had a shaved head, and I suppose that was one of the reasons I decided to sit with him. My own kind, I figured. Us shavers need to stick together. Maybe the choice to sit there was due more to his demeanor. If there had been a completely open double seat, I would surely have sat there by myself, however, looking at the thralls of sad-eyed, sunken-cheeked passengers that fill every Greyhound bus, Jimmy stuck out to me as someone who would ask no questions, and if need be, hold a decent chat. He also looked like someone I could talk out of his window seat.

After I explained to Jimmy that I hadn't been able to both take a ride and enjoy the scenery in the last 15 years, he didn't say anything. He understood. He just quietly stood up, collected his shit off the floor, and motioned me into what had just been his seat.

From Michigan all the way to Mississippi, Jimmy and I probably exchanged no more than 100 words between us, and most of those were to the effect of "burn one at the next stop?" Or, "got a rest area up ahead, grab me a soda while I go to take a piss." That sort of thing. Our small talk centered around the scheduled stops along the route. There wasn't much talking during the drive.

It wasn't until we crossed the Mississippi state line, that Jimmy pulled out his phone and solemnly dialed a number. There must not have been an answer the first time, because he whispered something to himself, then he calmly redialed. On the second try, I heard what sounded like an old man answer the phone. My assumption was verified by Jimmy, in a very low voice said, "Hey, Pop."

I could tell by the way he lowered his tone and shifted his position in the seat, that there was more to this than a simple call home to the old man. I have never been the kind to mind other people's business, so I did my best to keep my nose out of it. Finally, I got up, brushed past Jimmy, and trudged to the back of the bus, where there was a bathroom of sorts. More like a rest area toilet, with dumbass quotes written on the walls like: "I banged Hillary Clinton in Dayton, Ohio, now it burns when I vote." And that smell that lets you know this is definitely not your bathroom, but a dreary pit where piss and shit rumbles and slushes above the highway in an appalling tango.

As I neared the back of the bus, the door to the bathroom opened and a skinny-faced man who looked like he was in his late 50s stuck his head out. Our eyes locked, and I could sense that he was deciding if I was a threat to whatever he had going on in there. Nope.

He scanned the rest of the seats looking for the same threat from anyone else, and when he didn't find it, turned back around. A moment later, the door opened wide and he strolled out, followed by a woman with gray, spotted skin, and mat of tangled blonde hair. I remembered her from when I first got on the bus the previous day. She was sitting alone then, and I briefly considered sitting with her until I noticed the state she was in. She looked like a career dope fiend, except that she was missing that air of sorrow that often hovers above the junkie. She gave me the feeling that she would cut my throat without much thought in the act, and that just by looking her way I had endured more of her than I ever should have. Her whole aura was filthy and disturbing. At that point, I hadn't been laid in 15 years, but I didn't even want to be near this woman. That's when I noticed Jimmy and decided I'd sit with him.

As the old man and this woman exited the bathroom, I realized what time it was, and I froze on the balls of my feet. "Godammit, Jimmy," I thought. "You had better appreciate the privacy." The plan was to grab a toke or two while he made his call. I didn't want to go in that bathroom, but to hell with it, at least I got a decent chuckle out of some the writing on the walls, left there by these modern marker-wielding poets.

By the time I got back to the seat, Jimmy was just wrapping up his phone call. When he saw me standing there, he cocked his head up sideways, at the same time he wiped away a tear from his right eye. I almost missed it, but a change in his posture had made me look closer. He had lost some of that calmness and was sitting rigid in his seat. As I scooted past him and sat back down, I had the strong impulse to ask him if he was ok. Hell, things between me and my old man aren't all that great either. I let the thought pass, though, and instead asked Jimmy if he wouldn't mind letting me use his phone to make a call of my own.

"Sure," he said. And handed the thing over to me.

"Uh, this is a little embarrassing." I said. I wouldn't even know how to turn this machine on."

"What do you mean?" He asked me suspiciously. Probably thinking I was messing with him.

"Dude," I shot back. "I've been in the joint for a while. Long years. I've never even seen a phone like this before. You get the internet on that thing? Good grief, the times have changed."

"Oh," he said. "I didn't know. Sorry."

"You're all right." I assured him. "It ain't shit. Just dial this number for me."

I noticed Jimmy never asked me one single question about prison after that. I knew I sat with this guy for a reason.

Kim answered on the third ring.

"Hello," she said in that sweet southern voice of hers, the voice that over the last five years had come to be medicine to me. We had started writing to each other when a friend of mine had set me up on some website that puts prisoner's information out there for anyone to see, in the chances of finding a pen pal. I didn't even know I was on there until the guard slid her first letter under my door. Nice fellow, my friend. Must have cost him an hour's pay to do that for me.

"Hey there, gorgeous," I said, as I usually did when I would call her from prison.

"Charlie, is that you?" She asked. She must have been confused, since all the calls I had ever made to her before started with a recording stating that it was from an inmate, informing the caller, and the callee, that the conversation may be recorded and so forth.

"Yeah, it's me. I hate to surprise you like this (I didn't), but I figured I had better let you know that they cut me loose, and I am headed to New Orleans like we talked about."

After a long silence she said, "You're out?"

"Yeah," I replied, sensing apprehension in her tone. "I am headed your way, you don't sound too excited."

"No, I am, you just caught me off guard. I thought the parole board gave you an 18-month flop."

"They called me back early. I finished a class on time, and they called me back. Kicked me out of the door."

In retrospect, I should have read the thing for what it was. I know that tone. The one that instantly transports an ignorant goof like me from the inside to the outside, only to be left looking in with drooling lips and a fixed stare.

No way! I quickly put the thought out of my head. This woman has been with me through the last five years. We have a bond that is stronger than steel. How many times have we talked about the day I was out of the joint? How I would come get her, and we would go carve out our own corner in the mountains of Alaska, my old stomping ground. Where we would nibble on the crumb. *Five Years*. No. Surely that tone is just one of surprise; she wouldn't waste her time like that.

"Are you there?" I asked.

"Of course, I am. I'm here for you." Ok, that was better. She was putting my doubts at bay now.

"So, yeah, I'll be at the Greyhound terminal in New Orleans tomorrow around 7:30 pm. Are you going to be there?"

"Yeah, I'll be there," she said.

"Alright, I'll see you there then, and Kim… "

"Yeah?"

"…I love you, have a good night."

"You, too."

I handed the phone back to Jimmy. "You turn it off, buddy. Thanks."

"She won't be there." Jimmy suddenly said, out of nowhere.

"What the fuck! What are you talking about?" I snapped. As if I didn't know he had been sitting right there listening to the whole conversation.

"I ain't trying to sound like an asshole, bro, but she's pulling the okee-doke on you. I seen it before, shit, I done it myself to a couple broads. They do it to us, too. You been in the joint; your head's all screwed up with a woman. She was just passing the time with you my friend. Sorry, but I know. It's been done to me. I've done it myself. Just human nature, to pass the time with someone."

"No," I said. "You don't know Kim. She's one of a kind. I never met a woman as good as her."

"You've been in the joint man," Jimmy said. "Just think about it. Your head ain't right concernin' a woman."

"What do you know about it? Have you been in the joint before?" I asked.

"No, I just know humans. She was passin' the time with you. You probably made her feel good about herself. Here's this guy, listening to her and letting her be herself, so she gets wrapped up in it. Probably thought you'd never get released, or that you would fade away with the years. And she wouldn't have to ever tell you the truth, that you were just a way to pass the time. Think about it. When you were a teenager chasin' muff all over the place. You didn't care as long as you got what you wanted, right? But those broads you were passin' time with, they probably didn't see it that way. And you knew it, and you didn't want to tell 'em otherwise, didn't want the bullshit sure to come from telling them. So, you let 'em figure it out on their own, just like ole girl there is doin' to you right now."

Sweet Jesus! That was some serious dope Jimmy just laid on me. Somehow, I thought he might be right, but in a way, I felt, he was dead wrong. I had to give this one a heavy think.

"Anyway," he broke back in, "I am getting off in Biloxi. I need to get some sleep. Do you want to go back there and smoke a joint?" He motioned at the back of the bus toward the bathroom.

I thought about what I had seen, or rather, what I had assumed I had seen earlier.

"No, I'm good I don't want anyone to get the wrong idea."

"What?" He asked.

"Nothing, forget about it. I'll wake you up in a couple hours so you can get yourself together. You meeting your old man at the terminal?"

"Naw, fuck him. I'm going to meet my woman. She's got a house right outside Biloxi. I am going to pump a couple kids in her and work in the cement factory."

"Just passing time?" I asked.

"Might be, might be. Could be that's what she's doin' too, who knows?" He said this with the impish grin of a crooked judge. It made me think of all the mean-hearted people I had ever met.

"Well, Jimmy," I said, "you turned out to be a real dicksucker. I'll wake you up outside of Biloxi."

We rode on for another hour or so. I sat there in my seat, watching the scenery fly past my window like a beckoning spirit. Every sight I saw looked like some place I would rather be. When the edge of the highway was nothing but trees and bushes, I wished that I could pick any spot among their outer perimeter and penetrate their thickness, armed only with a fearless sense of adventure; ready to accept anything I may encounter while exploring the deepness beyond. I was hit suddenly with the realization that, yes, nothing was keeping me from doing so. No armed guards or electrified fences. I could stop this bus right now. Yell some crazy babbling bullshit at the driver. Terrify the hell out of my fellow passengers. Then I would be kicked off this vehicle right there beside that unknown forest. I doubt he'd just pull over and let me out now on the side of the highway if I simply asked nicely.

I could head into those woods, forget everything. Forget Kim, forget my family, forget the last 15 years… It would certainly be a journey. However, one thing kept my sudden fantasy in check. The thought of what awaited me in New Orleans. I didn't want to forget about Kim, no matter what I told myself. The phone call had left me edgy and unconfident, yet I had to be sure. For the promise of that adventure was worth the risk, the chase. If I ended up on my face in the dirt, then I might be able to convince myself somehow that I enjoyed the fall.

I was jerked away from my trip by a sign that informed the drivers that Biloxi was 10 miles away. Jimmy was still asleep, so I quietly said his name.

"Better not shake this boy awake," I thought. He has some demons buried deep. I was sure of it when he laid that mess on me about passing the time. Had he been screwing with me? Was he lashing out in some passive aggressive way because I had seen him cry? I couldn't be sure. Better wake him up softly. A bus full of degenerates and junkies would be a perfect target for the next mass-shooter. If that's what was to go down sometime in the next 10 miles, I want Jimmy to remember that I woke him up nicely.

"Huh," he half mumbled as he straightened himself up and rubbed his face roughly.

"Ten miles, buddy. Where's the cement factory?"

"What? Factory? He seemed confused. Then his eyes cleared and I saw the familiar look of someone remembering a lie they had told and been called out on. "It's on the West end of town. Why? You figure on sticking around here, getting a job with me?"

"Nope," I said. "I wouldn't want to blow your cover."

"My cover?" He asked, a look of suspicion on his face.

"I'm just fucking with you, man. Say, you don't have an AR-15 in your bag, do you?"

"What? What are you talking about?"

"Nothing," I replied. "I am going to press on. I was supposed to stay in Michigan for my parole. I am headed to Alaska one way or another. I grew up there. They won't find me if I bury myself deep enough in the mountains. Just need to stop by Nola's first."

"I told you she ain't going to be there," He shot back quickly.

"You're starting to piss me off." I said. "Why are you burning bread on me?"

"Look, man, I don't mean to upset you. I just know how it goes. I heard you on the phone with her. I can tell you love her. And that's just what I am saying; the way a person feels about another, it's never returned by the one they feel it for. I've been around long enough to know that."

I said, "You're a pretty cynical son of a bitch, aren't you? What about this woman you supposedly have waiting for you just up the road?"

"That's just my point," he replied. "She loves the hell out of me, but I don't have much of the same for her. She thinks I do, but I don't. I don't dislike her enough that I can't stand her, but at the same time, I can take her or leave her. Any way things go, I know she loves me. And I can always be sure that I have a roof over my head, and a warm body lying next to me at night. So what? If I ever get tired of her, she can figure it out on her own. What do you think I'm doing on this bus?"

"I don't know," I answered.

"Well, I'll tell you. I was up in Delaware getting my heart torn out by the broad that I love. I thought I'd go up there and surprise her, and wouldn't you know it, she let me figure that one out on my own. That's how I know. She was just passin' time with me. Three years I've known her. This one here in Biloxi, she never knew about the other one. I met her when she was down here visiting her family. She went back up north last year. I figured I'd squirrel away some cash, go up there, and surprise her. I was the one that got the surprise though. We had been keeping in touch the entire time, but when I went up there and saw her, I realized she had been using me to kill the time."

I sat back and let what he had just told me sink in a bit. After a few moments I said, "Jimmy, you are one sorry sack of sheep shit. But I like you. I hope you can make it work here with this girl you don't care about. I hope those kids you plan to pump her full of never know just what a sheep-shit old man they have. Thirty years from now, when one of them calls you on the phone, I hope they are able to hide their tears better than their father. Remember what I said though, I like you all right. I know lots of jack assess, get a kick of all of them. Hey look, Biloxi Greyhound Terminal. This is your stop."

He looked at me sideways, and for a moment, I thought I might have a fistfight on my hands, but Jimmy just nodded in a way that said he knew what he was talking about, that I was the jackass, and stood up. He bent down and collected his bags from the floor. As he slung one of them over his shoulder, I saw something fall out and land on the seat. It was shiny, and when it hit the seat, it rolled to the backrest and wedged itself in the crack. It took a second for me to realize what it was. A fucking bullet! .223! I was positive. Sonofabitch! He quickly reached down and scooped the round off the seat. I tried to act like I didn't know what I had seen, but when our eyes met, I saw that he knew. I shrugged my shoulders in a way that said I didn't give a shit about his business, and with that, Jimmy turned and walked down the aisle.

I watched out my window as Jimmy stepped off the bus and was met by a woman with long, brown hair that bounced as she trotted excitedly toward him. I was stunned; she was absolutely beautiful. She had on a pair of faded jeans and a black T-shirt that showed her figure off in a very powerful way. I could tell by the way she smiled at him that Jimmy was the center of her world. How this lameass could not give a damn about this woman, I did not understand. For a brief second, the primal urge all men have, whether we admit it or not, struck me, and I envisioned myself getting off the bus, killing Jimmy and slinging this woman over my shoulder like a horny Cro-Mag. Save her from a life with this loser. I wondered if she knew what his little trip up north had been about. Hell, after seeing that bullet drop out of his bag, I had to wonder myself.

I sat quietly and watched while she and Jimmy walked over to a nice looking and well kept up Dodge, got in and tore out of the parking lot of the Biloxi Greyhound Terminal.

New Orleans didn't go so great. Now it's on to Phoenix. I have to make one last stop before I can set my sights on Alaska. I wasn't planning to travel this far into the desert, but like I said before; once I enter into that state of not giving a damn, I have the tendency to push it as far as I can. Until I am either stopped by my better self, or by some other entity that is beyond me in strength and numbers, which usually means the Police. And I had left my better self with Kim in New Orleans.

I knew as soon as I got off the Greyhound and looked into her eyes, that Jimmy, that motherfucker Jimmy, was at least halfway right in his mad philosophy about passing time. Right away I sensed that things with Kim were foul. The way she looked down at her feet when I walked toward her, the way she hesitated when pulled her in for a kiss. It was as clear to me as if she had tattooed it on her forehead; the last five years had been a waste of time. What a fool I had been. Who was I kidding? How could I ever expect to keep a woman in my corner with nothing but visiting room embraces, and nightly telephone calls. Letters written during the late boring hours, paragraphs of lovely bullshit and misleading thoughts. What we were confronted with here was real, and I could see that for her, this was too real. She wasn't expecting this man to actually materialize into her world. She had been comfortable just passing the time, and anything else was my own delusion.

I was able to get her to admit that much to me. I was also able to coax out of her the name of a man living in Phoenix, who she has been in a serious relationship with for the past year. Of course, she had been meaning to tell me this, she was sorry. She would always value our friendship and other garbage you say to someone in these situations.

I didn't have enough spite in me to tell her that this guy she called Thomas, could not possibly give a damn about her, was only passing the time. And that Tom more than likely had himself somebody else there in Phoenix that he was fixated on. I wanted to lay Jimmy's gag on her, to let her know what was what, but I was so disheartened at that point, that I couldn't muster the words. I wanted to tell her that I would love her no matter how she felt about me, that I could be there always, to be a warm body in the bed, and someone to share the roof over our heads. That thought disgusted me though, and I quickly put it aside. Instead, what was growing in my heart like a poisonous shrub was the overwhelming primeval urge to see revenge. In whatever way happened to strike my fancy in the heat of the moment. Not to prove any kind of point, yet to soothe my ego after it had suffered this savage beating.

After playing it off to Kim as though she hadn't just ripped my guts out through my asshole, I calmly invited her to get a sandwich at a nearby deli I had noticed on the way into New Orleans. We had, after all, known each other for five years, and I had convinced her that no matter what she felt, we could at least sit down and have a meal and talk for a while. I told her that I would be pushing on to Alaska just as soon as I could get a bus ticket, no hard feelings.

While we were waiting for our orders to be filled at the deli, Kim said she needed to use the restroom, and that is where I spied my opportunity. She had left her purse, phone and car keys on the table we had chosen to sin at. I quickly snatched everything up and headed out to the parking lot. The driver's side door to the Blazer was unlocked and I jumped in, sliding the key into the ignition.

"So long, Kim," I said to the air as I fired up the engine and pulled out into the street. My only thought was on how to find the interstate and head west.

So now it is that I am nearing Phoenix, with that ominous sunset to guide me, and an overriding sense of justice in my heart. I have broken parole in Michigan, I am driving a stolen car, and I am going to kill the first sonofabitch I come across in Phoenix with the unfortunate luck to be named Thomas. Guilty party or not. I may make it to Alaska yet, but I doubt it. My fate has been changed with the arid desert wind; my crumb has become smaller yet. No great weight for a crawling ant like me to carry. Since, after all, I am only passing the time.

Christopher Marek
Graceland

The first time I heard "Gumboots" by Paul Simon, Chatter pointed to
the boombox bungee-corded to the dash with one hand on the wheel.
I smiled across the cab of the truck and said, "This is like my personal
message to Kelly Kapowski. Remember her, Brando?" Then—and this is
where it gets hazy—suddenly I could no longer see the horizon line ahead
of us. I could no longer see the fuzzy heat coming off the road like long-
ignited coals, but stared through the windshield at the full sun, a breath-
stealing thunderclap erupting beneath us—all of this outside of Fallujah,
Iraq.

*   *   *

"There are people in there—lots of them," Denise said and pointed from
the driver's seat of our parked car in the driveway to our unlit bungalow,
half-masked by the dark winter night. "I just think you should know that."

I laughed from the passenger seat. "What do you mean—there are
people in there?"

"It's supposed to be a surprise welcome-home party: pick you up from
the airport, walk you into the house, everyone jumps out from behind the
sofa, runs in from the kitchen, and shouts, 'Welcome home, Brandon!' I
liked the idea," she said, and I could sense her sudden pensivity. "I did,
but now that we're here, it scares me. It worries me." Denise placed her
hands back on the steering wheel and squeezed. I watched as her knuckles
turned white. "I'm worried it might be too much too soon," she said in a
small voice. "You've been through a lot."

"Denise," I said. "I'm fine." The truth is, I didn't know what to say. The
happiness and excitement from the airport and the ride home—elation of
just being able to see each other and touch each other and be in the same
country as each other after so long apart—seemed to have deflated, and it
caught me off guard. Did she really think that, I wondered, that a surprise
party might be more than I could handle?

"Brandon," she said and reached for my hand.

"Yeah?"

"There is a dog in there, too, a German Shepard," she said.

"A dog? A dog is fine. Who brought a dog?" I asked and hoped she
didn't somehow think I may be afraid of dogs now, too.

"No one brought a dog, Brandon. I adopted one. We've always
talked about it, and I thought now would be a good time. I read about
soldiers who get hurt or have traumatic experiences and how the VA and
other groups have been giving them dogs to, you know, cope with what
happened. I know you're not a soldier, but you were over there. And after

what happened, I just thought a dog might help."

"Denise, I don't know what you think, but I'm okay, really," I said and squeezed her hand. I looked through the dark at our house, the house we had shared for close to 10 years, the house I had seen little of in the past two, and suddenly realized that I didn't want to go in, not because I didn't want to see the people waiting inside, but because I didn't want them, my friends and family, to look at me like Denise looked at me now—like I was broken.

"I didn't name him yet," Denise said. "Maybe we can pick out a name together."

"The VA gives service dogs to soldiers with PTSD, and I don't have PTSD. And you don't even like dogs. What are you going to do when I go back?"

"What do you mean—go back?" Denise said in disbelief. "Do you really think you're going back there?"

I could feel my shoulder on the pillar of the car, my thigh pressed against the console, my elbow squeezed against the door panel, and the closing proximity of the headliner. Of course, I'm going back, I thought.

*   *   *

Grumman-Hobart, the defense-services contractor I worked for, prohibited listening to music on transports. Have to be ready, they said, always aware, and the dashes of the garbage trucks we drove all had black holes filled with loose wires where the factory AM/FMs had been. Every team took radios anyways though. You almost had to just to break up the monotony of 15 or 16 hours of continuous driving, of staring at nothing but the hot sun and the debris that littered the broken roads. Most civilian drivers I knew drove through the half-sand-covered roads blasting Metallica or 10-year-old rap music, boomboxes velcroed to the seatbacks. These were the high-octane, waiting-to-die, Redbull-slamming, hands-clenched-to-the-wheel guys, the guys who thought they were active combatants in a war, not civilian contractors making 40 grand a quarter hauling loads of trash to G-H burn pits to be ignited with jet fuel. These were the kind of guys who, sitting at home with a new suitcase between their legs, pack five bulletproof vests and two pairs of underwear. Chatter and I were not these guys. We weren't. Chatter, on his fourth re-list, sold his own Grumman-supplied vest on eBay, reported it stolen, got another one from the company, and sold that one, too. My vest sat unpacked in the barracks, five months into a six-month deploy. We didn't need to slam energy drinks or listen to heavy metal to summon the courage to do our jobs or try to grow mustaches like the Army Delta guys. We knew the deal; as long as we didn't act like idiots, we were safe. We knew it.

*   *   *

Denise and I met playing bar-league softball. A 19-year-old nursing student, Denise played second base for her dad's excavation and demolition company and turned a plain softball uniform into a sight of wonderment and awe. I played shortstop for Abbot's Tavern. I was a 21-year-old, almost-burnout who ran the bases with reckless abandon because Jim Abbott's favorite player was Pete Rose, and I hoped—prayed—the extra hustle might equate to more than just the one free pitcher after the game. Denise came to bat in the bottom of the second inning, got in her low-to-the-ground, Rickey Henderson-like stance and hit the first pitch hard on the ground to my left. I quickly sidestepped to get in front of it and watch the ball into my open glove—or at least that was the plan. The ball, coming fast in the warm afternoon sun, nicked a stray infield stone and skipped up high just before reaching my glove.

"Just get up," is the first thing I thought after Denise's hard-hit ball clomped me on the head. Maybe I could jump up, find the ball, and still make the throw to first.

Maybe I could avoid the embarrassment of being hit by the ball. Maybe nobody even saw what happened, I thought. Maybe I could play it off like it wasn't a big deal. I just had to get up.

So I did. I quickly jumped off the ground, looked for the ball, felt woozy, realized getting up was a mistake, lost my balance, and fell back down again. I stared up at the spinning blue sky above me, my head throbbing with pain, and the first person who appeared above me was Denise, an apparition with her red hair softly blowing in the wind.

"You are so beautiful," I said to her from my back.

"Brandon Parker," she said, peering down at me. "I believe you have a concussion."

Maybe I did, but Denise and I married eight months later. And after 12 years of marriage, the entire time I was in Iraq, when I thought of her, I thought of her standing above me on the field, staring down at me like an angel. It wasn't all perfect—our life together. But some of it was.

*   *   *

I came across the ad in the newspaper while eating breakfast. "CDL Drivers Needed for Overseas Transport," it read. "Top-Dollar Paid." I had long heard that defense contractors paid big money to civilians willing to work in or near war zones—Iraq, Syria, Afghanistan. I had no real desire for a new job; I had worked for Denise's dad since a month after we met. I felt curious, though. How much is "Top Dollar," I wondered? In between bites of buttered toast and sips of coffee in our half-lit kitchen, Denise still upstairs sleeping, I folded the paper around the ad, creased it, neatly tore it out, and put it in my pocket. Maybe I would call later—just to find out.

But I didn't. I forgot about it, and when I emptied my pockets on the dresser before jumping in the shower after work, the now wrinkled ad sat in a pile of change.

As I kneaded shampoo into my hair, warm water spilling on my back, I heard the bathroom door open. "Honey, what's this?" I heard Denise's voice ask.

"What's what?" I said as I peeked out of the shower curtain to find Denise sitting on the fuzzy toilet lid in our cramped bathroom with the ad in her hand.

"Are you looking for a new job? Is something wrong at work?"

"That's for a truck driver, overseas—probably in Iraq or Afghanistan," I said over the shower water. "Remember, we saw that *Dateline* episode about a diesel mechanic earning, like, 200 grand a year working for a defense contractor? I think that's the same thing. Things are fine at work. I thought about calling to see what 'Top Dollar' really is. I'm just curious. That's all."

Her tone changed from one of worry to one of wonder. "I remember that," she said. "Ha! We should call."

That's how I got the job. We called and Grumman-Hobart sent a representative to the house—they insisted on it. But when he came, he asked the questions: What were my qualifications? Did I have a passport? Arrest record? And when it came time for us to ask the questions, the rep couldn't help us. We would need to sign a privacy agreement, he said, first. Then a physical was scheduled—just to see if I was fit. I didn't want the job. I didn't, but this was our adventure, Denise's and mine, so I went. I could always tell them later that I wasn't interested—if Grumman-Hobart even offered me a job.

A few weeks later, Denise called me during lunch and told me an envelope had arrived in the mail from Grumman.

"Inside is a plane ticket—a fucking plane ticket, Brandon! Did you take that job without talking to me? Did you?"

"No, I didn't take the job," I told her. And I didn't. I mean, did I? There was no offer, no handshake, no yes.

Two weeks later I left for Iraq. I went because of the confusion, because I felt responsible for it. I went because this absurd hypothetical suddenly seemed logical. I went because of the bonus check that came with the plane ticket.

*   *   *

After the attack—after the IED—I woke up in a hospital room. My mouth and the entire length of my throat felt like sun-baked dirt. I didn't care that the fluorescent lights above me were too bright, that tubes and wires seemed to emanate from every part of my body, that the white cinder block walls were hung with signs I couldn't read, that some skinny kid with the a too-tight polo shirt paced the waxed red brick floors ahead of me, that I didn't know where I was, that I didn't understand what happened, that I didn't know how I came to be there, that everything seemed viewed as if through some stranger's prescription glasses. I didn't care about any of it. I just wanted water. I needed it.

"Whaaa," I said. "Whaaa." It came out like a guttural grunt.

Polo shirt stopped, pivoted, and focused on me. "Morning, champ," he said. "I knew you'd be fine, even if you had us worried for a moment." I could just make out the Grumman-Hobart badge hanging around his neck. He couldn't have been more than 23.

"Whaaa," I said again, still unable to make the second syllable.

He didn't understand. "What happened?" he asked. "What happened is that you're going to be fine. And what's important, Brandon, is that Grumman-Hobart is going to take care of you—remember that."

"Whaaa," I said. "Whaaa!"

I was in a hospital in Damascus because Chatter and I had been hit by an IED three and a half days ago en-route to the Grumman burn pits. Investigators believed it had been concealed in the road and detonated by an insurgent with a clear view of our approach. An army recon team found us, the truck overturned and me 20 feet away from what remained of the truck and Chatter's remains. His funeral would be held tomorrow, back home in Chesapeake. I sustained a grade-something brain trauma, lacerations to my chest and face from going through the windshield, and burns to my neck and arms—not from the explosion itself but from sun exposure. We weren't found until close to seven hours after the attack. I had been in a medically-induced coma since my arrival here. This is what Polo Shirt stood there and told me, but all I could focus on was my painful, scabbed-over-feeling throat and mouth. And at some point, in between olive-skinned nurses and doctors checking my pulse and blood pressure, shining lights in my eyes, and speaking a language I recognized but didn't understand, Polo Shirt put his too-big cellphone to my ear and told me someone wanted to speak to me.

It was Denise. In between crying and gasping she said, "Are you okay, Brandon? No one will talk to me. I call the hospital, and no one speaks English. I call Grumman, and all they want to talk about is a radio—a radio Brandon."

"Whaaa," I told her. "Whaaa." I didn't care about brain trauma or IEDs or funerals or Damascus or radios. I just wanted water.

*   *   *

I felt like I was accomplishing something in Iraq, that I wasn't just getting by. I took the job at 31, and up to that point, my life passed by in a flash of sameness. I became aware, in the time I worked there, that if

I hadn't taken the job, my life would still be flashing by. I would still be imprisoned by my daily tasks and thoughts, the minutiae that made up my life. She would never admit it, but Denise liked it, too.

"Where is Brandon?" her friends and coworkers would ask.

"In Iraq," she would say. I was no longer just her husband, I think, her husband that delivered excavation equipment and demolition debris for her dad and always had, this too-familiar husband that didn't quite live up to all of her expectations, that let life get boring, that not only forgot he had dreams, but forgot what a dream was. I was this new and exciting thing: a husband with a dangerous, high-paying job in a foreign country. I had done something different. I broke the mold.

But after the attack, living in the reality of it, I'm not sure if either one of us wanted to continue on the current path or backtrack to the old one.

*   *   *

I woke to the explosion erupting beneath me, the G-force of it shocking my body taut, to the 12-ton garbage truck spinning upwards away from the earth. I woke to the overwhelming sun replacing the road through the shriek of unbreakable steel bursting apart in the desert heat.

And I woke to my bedroom, to the soft familiarity of my sheets, and the ceiling fan spinning slowly overhead. I woke to my heart thumping frantically against my chest, sweat beading down my face, and to my lungs devoid of air from screaming.

I realized I was still screaming, that I hadn't stopped. I could hear the reverberation of it, the internal echo. I could feel it pouring out of me.

I woke to Denise standing over the bed, her shaking hands held over her mouth in panic and tears streaming down her cheeks. I woke to the dog standing guard next to her, his ears pointed up, and his tail arrow straight.

"I don't... I didn't... Brandon," she stammered. "I didn't know if I should wake you up. I didn't... Brandon, what were you dreaming about?"

I took a deep breath and closed my eyes. I saw the Iraqi landscape flashing by the passenger seat window. I saw Denise's angelic face peering down at me on that softball field. I saw the ground evaporate beneath the wings of a plane on my first flight over.

"The Bengals," I said. "The Bengals were in the Super Bowl, and the quarterback... I dreamed that Andy Dalton threw interception after interception. I dreamed... "

*   *   *

For two years, on the first and fifteenth of every month, I could log into my checking account, and by mid-morning EST, I could see the Grumman-Hobart payroll deposit, but leaning against the breakfast bar at home, three weeks after returning home, I suddenly couldn't. I waited, I read an article about the new school millage, I took the dog out. I put a load of laundry in the wash. I came back, leaned against the breakfast bar again, re-typed the password, and still didn't see the deposit. I poured a glass of orange juice and took small sips. I hit refresh. I still couldn't see it.

I fished the Grumman-Hobart business card out of my wallet, dialed the number, and navigated the automation. I waited on hold. I waited and waited and waited, and then I finally heard a human voice on the other end of the phone. I told them my payroll wasn't deposited.

"Mr. Parker," the voice said. "You aren't eligible for pay while on disciplinary suspension."

It must be a mistake, I thought, an error, something the could be remedied. "I'm not suspended," I said. "There must be some mix-up. I'm on medical leave."

"Mr. Parker, I'm looking at it right here. You are on disciplinary suspension, pending investigation."

Later that day, the mailman delivered an envelope from Grumman, an itemized bill—$61,000 for emergency flight services, travel expenses, medical expenses, and a whole laundry list of other things, all neatly listed.

Denise immediately called an attorney.

*   *   *

The Iraqi nationals always offered up their cigarettes if they knew a contractor or soldier smoked. They were brown, acrid tasting things with no filters. "Take one please," they would say and act offended if you didn't. After smoking these things more than I would have preferred, Chatter let me in on the scheme.

"They are asking you to have one of theirs so they can politely ask for one of yours. American cigarettes are like gold here, Brando. They can trade your one cigarette for an entire pack of theirs."

I didn't care. I still smoked with them. I respected their ingenuity.

*   *   *

Denise insisted we take the dog to our appointment with the attorney. He could wait in the car, she said. It wouldn't take long.

"Is he helping?" She asked while I stood bare-chested, waiting for her to finish ironing my one good shirt.

Helping with what? I wondered. The dog was a big deal to Denise. I understood that. I was damaged from the attack, she thought, and the dog was the cure.

I didn't feel damaged, though. I thought about what happened. I did. I thought about Chatter only being 25, about how he bobbed his head in the cab of the truck, played drums on the dashboard, laughed, and made days and weeks and months of driving bearable. I thought about how he dominated the barracks ping-pong table, about the one time I tried to play him and how I couldn't even return his serve on account of the ball having so much spin on it. I thought about the girl back home he talked about, how he would clip her picture to the sun visor and look at it for hours as we barreled down the desolate Iraqi roads. I thought about how she had a boyfriend and only considered Chatter a friend. I wondered if she showed up at the funeral, and I thought about whoever planted the IED and what motivated him, if he smiled in glee when he hit the detonation button. It kept me up at night—these thoughts. And I didn't understand how a dog could help any of it.

"It would help if we could potty train him," I said as she handed me the warm shirt. Judging by the look on her face, it was the wrong thing to say.

*　　*　　　　　　　　　　　　　　　*

"You have been suspended for the duration of a misconduct investigation. Grumman-Hobart believes you violated company rules that resulted in the injuries to yourself and to a Mr... " our attorney said as he leafed through his legal pad on this dark stained desk. "...To a Mr. Chatman. They believe you were in dereliction of duty as the result of having a musical device—a radio, in this case—on transport, and they point to this as a contributing factor in the incident."

"Incident?" Denise stammered, sitting in the chair behind me. "My husband didn't have an *incident*. He was the *victim* of an attack." Denise was a thinker, and always calm resolver, and I had rarely seen her truly angry. But she seethed fury in that moment. "And Grumman has the nerve—the nerve—to suspend him? He is on medical leave. He is *supposed* to be on medical leave. He is insured by Grumman. He has been insured by Grumman. And they send us a bill for the injuries he sustained—like it's his fault. How is that possible?" she asked. "How?"

I couldn't process it, what the attorney said. They suspended me because of a radio—because Chatter and I had a radio? They blamed the attack on it?

"This is not a traditional, American-style legal situation, Mrs. Parker," the attorney said. "The disputed incident didn't occur here. It occurred in another country with a different legal system, and Grumman-Hobart isn't an American corporation either. As a result, almost any legal action brought against them wouldn't have jurisdiction in our courts."

"It's a hornet's nest," he said, and I will never forget that. He told us to wait for Grumman's official decision before pressing forward, that he would continue to look into it. Then he asked me if he could ask me a few questions. I fidgeted in my seat.

"Did Grumman-Hobart provide you with a list of rules that may or may not have covered their policy regarding musical devices on transports?"

I gripped the arms of the chair. "Um, they gave us a regulation packet before deploying, but I've never really read it. I don't think anybody does. It's, um, probably close to 40 pages long."

"Okay," the attorney said. "At the time of the incident—at the time of the attack—did you have a radio present in the vehicle, brought by either you or Mr. Chatman?"

Chatter always brought the radio. I mean, if he didn't, I would have. Everyone took a radio. It had nothing to do with the attack—nothing. It didn't cause it, and not having one wouldn't have prevented it. And... "

"No," I said. "We didn't have a radio."

"Grumman-Hobart has reported that the remnants of a radio were found in the truck, Mr. Parker. That's why I'm asking."

*   *   *

I knew she would ask, and she did. She spoke it softly from the passenger seat.

"Did you have a radio, Brandon?"

The still unnamed dog lay across the backseat with his head down, and a steady midwinter drizzle turned the dirty snow along the highway into a cold slush as we made our way back from the attorney's office.

I said nothing because I hoped that would be enough, because I hoped the question would go away, be forgotten. I didn't want to talk about a radio, about if we had one, about if it killed Chatter. I wanted to forget, to push it from my mind, to make it home, to find the bed, to block out the cruel dream with sleep.

"Did you? Did you have a radio?" Denise asked again.

I didn't answer. I focused on the road ahead, on the trees lining it, on the cars in the opposite lane speeding past us, on the people in these cars. Were any of their lives being torn down around them for something simple, for something they could have never guessed mattered? I wondered about this.

"I'm asking you—did you have a radio? Answer me!" She demanded. She screamed, and I could hear the break in her voice. "Answer me, or pull this car over right now!"

I did. I checked the rearview mirror and calmly hit the turn signal. I pulled onto the shoulder, and I sat there and told her. I told her that trash trucks don't get blown up, that insurgents target troop convoys, supply runs, and armament transfers, that the path to Allah is not paved by splattering 40 yards of ketchup smeared paper plates and week-old feces across the Iraqi desert, that this was a known fact. I told her that we had a radio. I admitted it. I told her that it didn't matter, that everyone had a radio, that it had no right to matter, that I was being blamed for a technicality that no one acknowledged until this very moment—this exact moment—in time. I told her that it wasn't my fault, that listening to a radio, a second-hand Sony CD player, did not increase an insurgent's willingness to engage in jihad, that Chatter and I were safe, that we had discovered this, that trash trucks don't get blown up.

'They don't,' I said. I felt the tears coming down my cheeks, and I watched as Denise unbuckled her seatbelt and opened the passenger door to the cold outside.

"But you did get blown up. You did," she said as she lifted herself off the seat and out the door. "I'm walking, Brandon. Don't come after me."

I didn't. I turned to look at the dog in the backseat and then at Denise, walking away in the rain. I closed my eyes and thought of Chatter, of this smiling face. I felt my heart beating through my shirt. I struggled to breathe and to push that thought, any thought, away. I turned on the radio.

"You don't think you can love me, but I feel you can," Paul Simon sang from the speakers.

I jumped out of the car. "Denise!" I screamed as cars flew past me. "Denise, who is Kelly Kapowski? Denise!"

All I could see were her soft footprints in the slush. She was gone. I got back in the car, closed the door, turned to the backseat, and asked the dog why did everything have to be so hard.

Steven L. Montez
Benny Before Us

"Did you tell them that my chest hurts really bad?"

Among the last words that Benny spoke behind these walls of razor and wrong were pleadings for basic relevancy among the human race. You may feel surprise at the dismissive nonchalance illustrated in the story that follows. But none of *us* do. Not anymore. It is my hope that you will also find your way through the shame and repulsiveness, outrage even, and see the wary splendor of the only grace so many of your brothers and sisters are afforded in these dark corners—in these clandestine crypts you and I have constructed to mask our consciousness and conceal our own right names. But this day there was simply a desperation felt fully only at the crossroads of stark mortality and lost liberty.

"Yeah, I told 'em!" barked the guard as he hung up with the nurse down in health services, not attempting to hide his disdain for this prisoner who was once so much more than a six-digit number. A paycheck. An interruption of this state employee's task at that moment—a task conveniently perceived as the priority. "But it's count time. So you're not going anywhere except back to your bunk! Go on!"

"But what did she say?" Benny implored.

"She said go lay down, and you'll be fine."

But he didn't feel fine. He felt the classic pains of cardiac arrest. He felt the physical symptoms. And also that innate fear of fatality. That voice in our heads that speaks in moments of trauma and distress to tell us that this is our official warning—to do something now or there may soon be nothing left to do. So after count, he went back to the guard and beseeched him to be allowed to try to walk down to health services, to be allowed to try to hold on to the only thing he had left. His life.

"It's shift change. You know there's no movement during shift change. Go wait until we call for you," was the inexplicably terse reply.

Two hours and fifteen minutes after Benny first reported his universally accepted dire symptoms, he was allowed to walk under his own power down the hill from his housing unit to the health services building in order to be seen by the nurse on duty.

She mock-listened to his description of symptoms, accused him of trying to get medicine that he was not prescribed—the implication being that he intended to either sell it to other prisoners or take it to get high—summarily rejected his concerns, and sent him back up to his housing unit. Protocol, along with the basic tenets of compassionate care, dictates that any prisoner experiencing the type of symptoms that Benny had be taken immediately to a hospital for diagnosis and treatment. But it is expensive and risky to transport an animal from his cage to a place that treats humans. There are so many important questions to ponder. What if he's faking it and just wants to take a ride through the free world and look at trees and cars and girls through the transport van's window? You know they're all liars. What if the extra paperwork keeps a staff member from going home on time after his shift? What if a fiercely guarded standard of dissociation is breached while packing up this internee's meager worldly possessions into duffle bags for storage until he is returned? If he is returned? What if he is accidentally humanized by a nurse who gently touches his shoulder and smiles and comforts him, or by a doctor who shakes his hand and calls him by his first name? What if his existence is shown mercy and significance? And finally, what if protocol is ignored? Who will know? To whom will it matter?

He climbed the hill, clutching his arm, grimacing in pain, gasping for breath. He almost made it to his bunk. But instead he collapsed on a stained blue carpet that stank of convicts' feet and aloneness, and drew his last breaths before fading into unconsciousness.

By this time, my loving wife, Barbara, was waiting down the lobby of the facility to be let in for our visit. It was Friday, and I was about to feel like a person, complete with purpose and inspiration, for a few hours in the healing arms of the one who helps me keep my breath in my own body. But first she watched them wheel Benny past the visitors to a waiting ambulance. Even unconscious, he was shackled and restrained. That is how it is done here, you know? Not even a parting modicum of dignity.

We sat together in the visiting room, a viscid pall resonating among the prisoners and their mortal host of witnesses, who have already endured too much worry and loss.

I broke the silence. "People die here all the time, baby."

But she surprised me by saying that she heard a couple of guards taking credit for saving his life by giving him CPR. Even as my spirit rolled with an indignant observation of the hypocrisy of those who work for the same disinclined system that contributed to this tragedy through aversion now taking credit for saving his life, I still had to acknowledge a pure and profound gratitude that maybe Benny hadn't died after all. Sometimes the only redemption for the crippling effects of disregard are actions whose grace is hidden beneath the mysterious layers of why things happen like they do. Maybe Benny was still alive. Was his salvation worth having to endure some culturally conditioned self-aggrandizement by the same entity that facilitated this unruly mess in the first place? Of course it was.

In the wake of this hopeful news, Barb and I spoke of Benny's recent disclosure to me that he had just been diagnosed with colon cancer. I reminded her that he had been one of the first to speak to me when I got here and found myself standing in line waiting for insulin, which he took as well. We talked about how he and I worked together in one of the few jobs that fit into the parameters of my personal moral code—packaging hygiene items for indigent and segregated prisoners. How he had just had a meeting with an advocacy group who was working hard to get him released for humanitarian reasons due to his diminished health. How he was a dedicated supporter of our band and could always be found sitting alone in the back row at our shows, clapping and smiling and going someplace less brutal than here for three and a half minutes at a time. Let them take credit for saving the man whom bureaucracy had proven content to bury. There was hope behind that hypocritical hubris. Maybe Benny was breathing right now, with a kind nurse gently touching his shoulder and a doctor shaking his hand and calling him by his first name.

But Benny wasn't breathing. And never would again. The next day I learned that although initial resuscitation efforts temporarily established some vital signs, Benny died a few hours later at the hospital. Alone. Chained to a bed. Because, as I may have mentioned, that is how it is done here. But finally and mercifully at home, in some abstract way, on the living side of these walls. Home, in some literal way, as his remains could now be unshackled and returned to his loved ones—if any still remained. Home, in some ethereal way, as his soul could now be enfolded in the arms of God—if such a thing exists despite the duality of our earthly struggle.

That night after music practice we said a prayer for our brother. I was surprised to learn that most of the guys in the group knew *of* Benny and his passing, but did not really know much more about him, including his support of our group and his love of music. But it didn't seem to matter all that much as we stood in a circle, hand in hand, with a palpable hopelessness in the air and a distinct pain in our own hearts that never truly stops anymore. We prayed in our own private manner among the million ways there are to do so. We didn't have to know him in order to *know* him. Each of us *was* him. In saying goodbye to Benny, we knew full well that we also said goodbye to one more piece of us that was left. It was not mourning per se. Sadness here struggles to stay inside defined lines, as individual sorrows merge to expand and sustain one pervasive grief. It was certainly not rejoicing as the recognition and celebration of life should be. Fear? No. Supplication? Not exactly. It was resignation. It was the only way we knew to acknowledge the only members of our human community who are doomed to be taken from this world twice. We knew that his fate would be shared by many of us. We knew that he was one of us and that his path would know our own footsteps in time. That the glory of our lives would one day know the bittersweet freedom of our deaths.

The miles and moments of the imprisoned man are a frantic search for some sublime meaning. Some recompense for a lifetime of faith that our worth is commensurate to the life and value and miracle of our creation. Some mortal quest to leave an immortal mark on something in this world that matters. Some universal language in which to say simply, "I lived" to a world that is diligently carrying out the task of forgetting.

Sometimes we search for salvation in praise and scripture, that we may one day hear the protective peal of heaven's voice. Sometimes we search for forgiveness from those who would have to forgive themselves first in order to hear us, that we may ease the futility of hoping to be fixed by the broken masses. Sometimes we search for the strength needed to walk down subjugation and indignity, that we may hold our heads high enough to see a cloud or a bird or another person's eyes and their mirror of our own. Sometimes we search for a song, a hand, a loophole, a good night's sleep, a change, a kindred spirit, a cause, a challenge, a chance, a view of something beautiful, that we may be reminded that we are still alive. And sometimes we all just search for a way home, like Brother Benny before us.

It sometimes feels like an eerily short time, but nearly a decade has passed since my days lost the wonder of a good wander. In those times, my very existence was a poem. Melodic and pastoral and bathed in free verse. Too common now are nights full of wakefulness and dread, contemplating the end of my story. Not fearing so much which words are written. Just that the last line is already down and too soon. Too soon. In short, my life has become the awaiting of one more paragraph, one more stanza, one more merciful word willing to take me back to yesterday that I may borrow from it hope for tomorrow.

And some days the only thing I can do is to throw sentences onto scraps of paper until I am reminded that for some reason I am still alive. Reflective essays about what made my life extraordinary. Ridiculous pieces about the absurdities of daily life that make my spirit laugh. Words about the joy of knowing beauty and freedom, and the trauma of having it all rent so brutally away. So until the past no longer finds me, and this day betrays the promise of the next, I will write. What more can a simple man do? Wait around for someone else to tell *their* version of my story? No. I will write. Until my journey is done, until my tale is told, until my story is over. I will write.

Deyon Neal
Conflicted

"You'll grow at a rate commensurate with your ability to perceive reality from both sides of the conflict you're in." The words were still echoing in my head as my cell door opened and I stepped out. I had just written them in a communication kite to a fellow prisoner named Meechy, whom I considered my brother. It was spiritual advice, my response in an intense, week-long discussion that we were having on paper about self-development. I walked through the metal detector downstairs, then out of the back door of my maximum-security cellblock onto the exercise yard, with our camaraderie in my heart, thinking, "Men sharpen men as steel sharpens steel."

A bright, mid-August, morning sun kissed me from the sky. I squinted downward from its beaming light while returning its warm greeting with a natural smile. A little after 9 a.m. and it was already muggy with promises of being uncomfortable later, but for now the humid air filling my nostrils and enveloping my body was quite pleasant. My lungs relaxed as I inhaled, inspired. I didn't need a reason to be happy. I was alive.

Our prison yard was an octagon no bigger than a corner store parking lot, loading with about a dozen preoccupied offenders ready to start their day; four middle-aged white men, one young Latino, and seven young blacks dressed in either white t-shirts and orange shorts or blue prison uniforms. Seven of them rushed to the six pay phones just outside the door to either place calls or make soap, deodorant, and coffee transactions from the previous day's bets. The two prison guards who formed the checkpoint that I had just walked past outside the doors were too busy performing random searches on the prisoners who were still coming out to catch the transactions being made with the contraband they missed.

The pull-up bars hadn't gone anywhere; two sets still stood empty near the corner bench that I headed to. The cell block's exterior, red brick wall was out boundary for half of the octagon. A 15-foot, metal fence with razor-sharp barbed wire at the top formed the other half of the yard's perimeter, binding us all in together, while the wall's dark windows of the first floor's calls, 11 on each side of the back door, mirrored our reality back as us. The wisest of us knew not to try looking beyond the reflection; it could get you stabbed for violating someone's privacy or flashed by the romancers who often put on masturbation shows for Katrina, the cell block's lone transsexual. Through the fence, about a hundred feet across the walk, sat the programs building, the healthcare building, and the chow hall building—all built with the same shape, size, and brick, probably by the same contractors.

There was no grass in sight, nothing green or organic, period; we had to look to the heavens for nature. The concrete beneath my feet had a few grimy puddles from last night's rain, as did the cracked, asphalt blacktop that made up the basketball court on the yard's right side. The foot-paved running track around the perimeter, which once contained grass, was all dust that made my black, state-issue, Oxford shoes look more rundown than they really were (I often avoided it if I wasn't exercising). John B., one of the few white prisoners, had already taken off jogging around it to the tunes of his Walkman. Probably rock. I wondered if it was that old Guns-N-Roses song that he was enlightening me about while leaving my red and black, cardboard chess set on one of the steel card tables for anyone who wanted to play.

I had no plans to, nor did I have any money left on my phone card to call home (the phones were taken anyway). Today was a no-exercise day, no pressure. I felt a little relief while sitting on the steel bench and looking back at the door for Tron, my workout partner. Tron was another prisoner whom I considered my brother. More prisoners poured out and the yard for much louder with chatter, laughter, and brotherly yelling. A semitruck engine groaned and beeped in the distance, probably somewhere behind the program's building. I exchanged greetings, hugs, and handshakes with Jose (the lone Latino), Blue (another considered brother), and L-Boogie (my other workout partner), then looked back up at the door again for Tron. He was finally walking past the guards.

Tron was twenty-seven years old with light-brown skin, dreadlocks, and the physique of a light-heavyweight boxer in training. He grew up "streetbanging" in Detroit's West 7 Mile neighborhood, now he wanted change. Nine years older, I took him under my wing earlier this summer. We planned to discuss the school that he dreamed of building for troubled youth, but when I read the uneasiness in his face, I knew that something else had become priority. He walked up and shook my hand.

"What up, bro?" I greeted.

"What up, though?" he greeted back in Detroit fashion with a tinge of dejection in his voice. "They probably 'bout to—"

Before the words even left his mouth, the center of the yard erupted. I heard it before I even saw it: *wack, wack, wack, wack!*—sounds of knuckles snapping against bare flesh. Who is… ? My mind asked and answered the question as my eyes locked in on Charlie's golden, bald head. His arms were launching fist-flurries, combination after combination at the head of—who is he fighting? I strained my eyes to zoom in on the other guy's face. He was swinging away too, a little slower, with his head turned away at an angle. A big dude. I mean, Charlie was big enough, about 200 pounds of solid muscle. (He was a former amateur boxer out of Flint, Michigan, who now worked out like a professional bodybuilder. Joking, I often called him Lee Haney because he had his shape.) But this dude that he was fighting was huge and fat: about 6-foot-3, 350 pounds of twirling blubber. The two bodies became a whirlwind of blue clothing and black flesh, a tornado of hatred that sucked in everyone's attention. Before I knew it, my blood was racing, and I was on my feet. Rushing adrenaline charged me with compelling motive force as I stopped breathing. Every atom of my body vibrated a hundred times faster, corresponding with the rapid rate and vigor of their performance. My hands had balled into ready fists, and I hadn't even noticed.

I looked around; first, to see if anyone else would move towards the brawl; then, to see who else was living out the experience in their physiology. Four dozen prisoners. No one moved except the two checkpoint guards, and they moved with pepper spray and tasers aimed: "Alright, come on, guys. Knock it off." Their first warning was passive, full of exhaustion and exasperation—just another day at the workplace. They lingered around the fight like tentative kids timing the rope of a double Dutch session, but they weren't about to break up the fight by themselves. Three more guards rushed through the door, providing backup. More confident, the passive guard ordered: "Okay, that's enough! Get on the ground, Austin!" Austin was Charlie's last name. He kept swinging. Brightmoor went down. Brightmoor! I finally saw his face when he rolled onto his hands and the fight rotated our way.

Named after his Detroit, Westside neighborhood, Brightmoor was a 23-year-old kid, doing no more than five years for a petty drug offense. He was maxing out his sentence next year, going home no different than he was when he came in. The small prison shank in his right hand said so. Someone stabbed my mom to death out in Brightmoor 26 years ago; she died fighting just as hard. He wasn't even alive when my fight began.

The shank didn't do much good against Charlie, but he held onto it tight while struggling to get back up onto his feet under Charlie's raining blows. One taser popped like a static, electric rubber band. Charlie swung on without flinching. A second guard fired his taser next. Charlie went down with Brightmoor, then they lay silent on their heaving chests and throbbing faces, practicing good prison etiquette (everyone knew to remain silent whenever things popped off on the yard) while the guards looked for the shank. Bright red blood trickled from Charlie's shiny bald head. Eight more guards rushed outside far too late. The fight lasted about 20 seconds.

My racing heart throbbed for a logical explanation. Tron waited until the guards led them away, spat in the dirt near the fence then addressed me.

"I was just about to say they was about to fight."

"What they get into it fo'?" I asked.

"Sellin' slum behind the door," Tron said. "Selling slum" was slang for exchanging insults and threats. Charlie and Brightmoor locked right across the hall from each other and argued all the time. Tron shook his head, sighing. "Charlie just got a 12-month flop, too… over some words."

I sat and wondered which words could possibly be worth a parole opportunity. In Michigan's penal system, a 12-month parole denial (we call them "flops") meant you had one foot out of the door; that if you stayed out of trouble for another year, your parole was certain. Charlie was also on his way home after serving 23 consecutive years. Brightmoor wasn't even alive when he got arrested for a robbery murder in the 90s, but somehow they had enough in common for Charlie, a 48-year-old man, to stand up in the door all day bickering about sports, crime, women, and entertainment with him. Until they fell out. Words create, heal, build, and destroy. If you're not discussing something productive, especially in this atmosphere, it will eventually lead to destruction— swinging fists and bloody shanks. I've seen it a million times during my 16 years in, which was why no matter how much I liked Charlie, I couldn't help resenting him for not knowing better.

For hurting me. I had 16 years left before the parole board even thought of me. I would've gladly traded shoes with him, so my disappointment was personal, like I'd just been slapped in the face. By ingratitude. Recklessness. Indifference. Despair. Senseless Black-on-black violence that we all should've been tired of. Self-hatred.

It tapped a well of trauma deep within me: How stupid? Wasn't even worth it. That little stuff? A 12-month flop gone for 20 seconds of release. They didn't even get any rec'. In the inner city, we fought uninterrupted for like 10 to 12 full minutes, until someone nearly died. This little stuff wasn't even an appetizer.

I stood there with my equilibrium shot, taking stock of each of my polarized thoughts, looking around at all of my potential enemies, four dozen: I wish one of ya'll would run up on me! I'ma try to kill one of y'all! Wow, I really thought that. I haven't had a good one in nearly 10 years. What if I'm rusty? What if the younger and quicker of them are thinking the same thing? And to think, we almost got through the summer with no fights. For those 20 seconds, they were free. Too free. I lamented, not just for Charlie and Brightmoor's misfortune, but for my own. As tired as I wanted to be of the madness, I still loved it.

Marcellus Earl Phillips
Lifesmithing

An old cliché states that figures lie and liars figure. I estimate somewhere between zero and 100 percent of the stories told in prison are hogwash. For instance, if you take the word of those incarcerated, nine of every 10 are innocent. But, this is all beside my point. What I want to discuss is the beauty of the clink. Unlike "Cheers," nobody knows your name. You are able to reinvent yourself with any identity you can imagine. The Army is limited to all you can be. In the calaboose, you can be all you can manufacture.

In 18 years, I have ran into only a handful of men from my hometown. It isn't a small burg and sits just outside of an urban zone that provides plenty of fodder for the justice department coffers. Still, only a few guys I've met knew people I knew within two or three degrees of separation. So, with no Google, who could fact check the background of anything I had chosen to tell everyone?

If I had the desire to convince the hoi polloi I was a highfalutin businessman, none would be the wiser. If I claimed to be the kingpin of my village, who could debate me? Granted, the fact that I am walking around mooching ramen noodles might cause some to wonder about my suspected hidden finances stockpiled in the care of a loved one.

By hitting the right pit or track, you can make quick strides to become what would appear to be a former high school superstar in the days of yore. Just look at the lineup of experts on ESPN who never played a day in the sports they expound upon, and you know you could convince a pack of sycophants you were once all state by breaking down the week's mistakes on television.

If I had wanted to be a Golden Gloves boxer or a cage fighter, who could argue the fact without engaging me in a bout of fisticuffs? Attempts to doubt my stories could be pounded into submission by informing them of the added risks I face if I were to use my hands to inflict any further injury. Therefore, part of my penitence is learning to handle myself without bullish physicality.

Be forewarned, getting caught in a military fabrication isn't as easily dodged as others. Those boys don't take their sacred oaths lightly. And, they know how to grill you into inaccuracies with their insider jargon.

To fulfill a drive to be a car guy, just relay anecdotes about growing up monkeying around in grease refurbishing classics with Dad. Who can refute how many hot rods we had in the garage? Plus, I can give you a list of my friends back home that will vouch for the fact I had NASCAR-level mettle with the pedal. The only thing that held me back was the politics of sponsorship connections.

Had I the appetency to expostulate on my extensive erudition, all I would have to do is emulate Oswald Bates from "In Living Color" by assimilating as many sesquipedalian lexical constituents as attainable. I could iterate Freudian ideologies, orate Shakespearean colloquy, and put on airs. Be not qualmish if you use them incongruously, the majority of this rabble will be awestruck at your audacity and the expediency with which you wield such linguistic refulgence.

Do you wish you had been married? Did you yearn to be more of a player? How about a pimp? Who's to say who you were involved with that have since decided to go their own way while you serve your time? They love me, so when I let them know I'm free, they'll be back.

When you're thrust into a new society with no familiar history or ties, what's to stop you from creating the most outlandish glory for yourself? Scruples? Integrity? We're talking about a collection of convicted criminals here. None of these examples, which are only the tip of the iceberg, are anything I've made up without having heard them ad nauseam.

In closing, I want to ask you a question: just how much stock do you want to put into anything I've shared with you here?

Jason W. Slaczka
Waiting on the Lord: A Memoir Excerpt

The segment which follows describes the inner conflict I struggled with when I couldn't reconcile things our pastor taught with my own experience. I hope it also suggests that little progress can be made through blind obedience.

We huddled on the family room floor, the four of us, still wearing our Sunday clothes. Sitting knee-to-knee we had been praying for two days and nights, so far.

I couldn't focus anymore. I had so many questions but tiredness kept yanking me into a fuzzy daze. I peeked up at Mom who sat across from me, her eyes closed, her lips whispering desperately for our sins to be washed white as snow. My legs had been asleep for so long I passed some time pretending this is what it would feel like to not have any. By this time tomorrow none of us would be here. We'd be with Jesus.

I imagined the landlord banging on our door, his mouth twisted tight like it got when he busted me fooling around in the basement workroom he kept at our house. He'd show up for sure when Mom didn't make the rent payment.

When nobody answered I knew he'd let himself in even though Mom gave him hell last time. I could hear the bark of his voice turn into a question when he found our emptied clothes on the family room floor like cold ashes from a long-dead fire.

But maybe Jesus would make us wear our clothes because being naked is a sin even though I can't figure out why. I hoped he'd at least let us wear our underwear. Thinking about how mad Mom got the time I busted in on her in the bathroom, I could only imagine how pissed she'd be if she had to be naked in front of Jesus and everyone.

When he found our clothes, maybe the landlord would be able to tell that Jesus had been there to get us, or maybe he'd even go to heaven, too. I'd seen the gold cross around his neck that was always tangled in his chest hair. I couldn't picture him naked.

We lived in an old farmhouse our dad said was all the way out in Bum Funny, Egypt whenever he came to pick us up. Since the divorce, we spent every weekend at his tiny apartment. He could be the one to not find us when he realized the world had been turned over to the devil just like we'd been telling him it would. But it made me sad to think about him.

He was still Catholic. Just from the way pastor spit out the word like it actually tasted bad I knew being Catholic must be somewhere between being a Satan worshiper and a practicing witch.

Once I'd become friends with a kid at school. We got close quickly because we were both desperate for friendship. I'd been to his house many times. His family was very poor and had to deal with an alcoholic father. Our friendship was terminated when someone in our church told my mom that his mom was a real live witch who even cast spells on people.

In our church Catholics were people confused by the devil into believing the Pope was God. In our church whoever didn't believe exactly like we did was being manipulated and blinded by Satan, and would burn in hell forever and ever, amen.

But for 1,000 years after the second coming of Christ, Satan would be allowed by God to rule the earth. I thought of dad fighting hordes of hungry demon people over scraps of food. Mom said it would be his own fault, that he'd been given the chance to ask Jesus to be his personal savior. She also said he'd have to repent for being loyal to the great whore, but I wasn't sure what she meant.

We made sure to ask him every time we spent the weekend if he was now ready for us to lead him in prayer so he could invite Jesus into his heart so he could go to heaven with us. But he always smiled and said maybe next weekend.

Pastor says Jesus will give everyone the chance to repent before He returns. It sounded fair. Then I thought about my baby cousin who was eight days old when he died. He looked like one of my sister's dolls laying in his tiny coffin. How would he have the chance to repent? And for what? When I asked my youth group teacher, he told me that all of mankind is automatically born into a sinful state because Adam ate the apple. It didn't sound fair to me anymore.

Pastor also says to have faith whenever something didn't make sense, that God would reveal His will to our limited understanding in his own time. But I was curious about everything and was a pain with all my questions. It seemed that the answers always circled back to just have faith. So to me have faith was another way to say I don't know.

All this thinking made me even more tired and hungry. Plus I had to pee. We knew at any second we would be raptured, so being away from each other was scary.

So we prayed about it and came up with a good way to use the bathroom. While one of us was in there, the other three stood outside the door while singing "Amazing Grace." This way, as long as there was still singing we knew He hadn't come yet. It reminded me of going Christmas caroling, only different.

After we all did "Amazing Grace," Mom let us munch on crackers and cheese. We all wanted something hot, but if Jesus came back in the twinkling of an eye before it was done cooking, then the house would burn down after we left.

We all went back to the family room where Mom told us to spend some time thinking about any sins that might still be staining our snow. It was important that we ask forgiveness quickly so God couldn't hold it against us and be forced to leave us behind. I had an idea to ask God to forgive me in general for any and all sins I'd ever done. Then I was afraid he would see it as being lazy, so I hurried to repent for that, too. It felt like I spent more time repenting than I did sinning.

Since we'd come home from church on Sunday we'd been on the lookout for Jesus. Now it was Wednesday afternoon, and my mind floated to what my friends at school would be doing.

We spent Sunday night praying non-stop, and when the sun came up on Monday, mom told us we wouldn't be going to school. I was excited, but after three days of waiting, I was ashamed that I'd rather be at school.

My friends would be in fifth hour, which was World History for me. But this only made me think about how after Jesus came for us, I wouldn't get to go to college and get laid, even though I was still piecing together exactly what the second part was. All I knew was I wanted to get whatever it was.

Pastor always told us we had to turn our backs on the things of this world and be grateful for the blessings of our salvation. But being grateful was hard sometimes. Like the Sunday when Pastor handed our wooden paddles to all the parents of our church. He said the Lord had impressed it upon his heart that the young people in his flock were not being sufficiently corrected, that God called upon him to make these paddles. He promised they were made with love.

The parents made their way down the center aisle toward the communion table where a stack of paddles were issued one by one. Etched into the beautiful table were the words: This do in remembrance of Me.

When the parents returned to their pew, some tried awkwardly to find a place to set the offensive wood, while a couple others tested its balance. Pastor told the young that we should be grateful that we had parents who loved us enough to chasten us.

Mom brought her paddle home that day and used it to prop open the bathroom window. It has been the paddle's place ever since.

I thought about a girl at my school who liked to wear shirts that had Bible verses on them, like Romans 1:16, which I won a candy bar for memorizing at youth group. Whenever she wore them, I was embarrassed. Kids would mock her, calling her Virgin Mary, even putting thumbtacks on her seat. But no matter what they did to her she would just smile like they'd done her a favor, and tell them that Jesus loves them.

I'd root for her secretly, but whenever I saw her surrounded in the hallway, I went the other way. I knew I should be standing right next to her just because we had the same Savior, but I knew also that I could never stand what she went through. She was the bravest person I knew. I hoped she would get the room she wanted in God's many roomed mansion. If she didn't, then I was stuck out of luck for sure.

Our family room looked like a Gypsy camp with all the bedding and Bibles. I'd tried a few times to crawl to my blankets and sleep, but I kept waking up afraid Jesus had left me behind. It reminded me of waiting for Santa, only with Santa I was excited. I was confused to be relieved as well as disappointed to jerk awake and still be there.

During Sunday service, Pastor promised that Jesus would return sometime before midnight on Wednesday. When he explained to the astonished church how he knew this, he handed out a small white booklet he said explained it in detail. He went on and on about Jewish holidays Rosh Hashanah and Yom Kippur.

I was confused because I could remember him saying to us whenever he thought we were up to no good that we had to be sure our snow was clean for we knew not when Jesus would come stealing back like a thief in the night.

Pastor asked if there were any questions, and a couple hands were raised. The questions he couldn't answer he said to just have faith, just have faith and wait on the Lord.

I knew what waiting on the Lord meant. It meant do nothing. It seemed people said they were waiting on the Lord when they felt helpless and it made that feeling tolerable.

One lady stood and said maybe we should all wait for Jesus together in prayer and celebration, but Pastor said no, that this was a time to spend with our loved ones.

I watched the sky through our family room turn purple and then black. None of us had said anything for hours. If anybody still prayed, it was from behind glassy eyes. My little brother was sleeping on his side in a corner.

I didn't realize I fell asleep until the shards of mom's sobs slashed into my sleep. I sat up to see my sister balled up in her lap. My brother now sat up staring at everyone. The clock showed 2:28. I looked out the window for the distant glow of fire I imagined must follow Satan wherever he went, but it was all darkness. All we could do was wait on the Lord.

James Stevenson
Silvery Lane

After months of deliberation Jack was finally the proud owner of a home with a cobblestone driveway. For him it wasn't so much the driveway, in fact it wasn't even the home that sat next to it. To be honest it was all about an elm tree positioned at the front of this lot that hung partially over the road.

Thirty years ago, this same tree was Jack's safe haven every Sunday and Thursday night. Jack would be sitting outside a restaurant waiting for Cassie to get out of work. About midnight she would come bursting out the door, then she would toss Jack the keys and say, "You're driving." Jack had expected as much, the passenger door was already open awaiting her arrival. After a quick kiss, he shut her door, then raced for the driver's seat of her used Buick. As soon as he pulled onto Telegraph she would hand him a paper bag that held a vanilla shake and large fries. This was Cassie's idea of distraction while she changed from her uniform into a faded pair of blue jeans and a shirt she confiscated from Jack a few months back. Sure the flannel has seen better days, but what it did have going for it was that it smelled exactly like him. Which helped Cassie sleep the other five nights that they weren't together.

Four miles, 10 minutes, and three turns later the Buick headed north towards a dark home, the one with the large elm out front. The shakes and fries had already become a memory as Jack turned the car and its headlights off. The next hour would be spent talking about their days apart, mostly it was spent complaining about their jobs. After that the next hour was spent exploring each other's innocence, then around 2 a.m. they would curl up together and fall asleep on the front seat of her small car.

At 5:30 a.m. chirping birds would always wake Jack, while his unembellished nightingale still slept soundly. Her kicked off shoes and socks littered the passenger floorboards, the top two buttons of the flannel were missing, while a lone gold chain and cross adorned her slim neck. Native blonde hair covered parts of her face and shoulders as "Love Bazaar" played softly from the back seat radio. For these two the words rang true, though to others they might be misconstrued. Four houses down a street light gave off an eerie glow as fog ran down the inside windows.

Outside rain gently moved across the glass. Looking up through the sunroof it seemed heaven had arrived, as their reflection hung proudly like a Rembrandt for all the world to see. This morning was for Jack's eyes only.

Jack could feel her heartbeat in his hand as her slow breath fluttered like a cool breeze upon his neck. Jack leaned in and kissed her sanguine lips gently, a hint of strawberries was still evident. Her blue eyes remained closed, covered by sea-blue eyeshadow. Here serenity was somehow achieved on the front seat of a Skylark, and that's exactly what happened every time they spent a night under their old tree. Outside of Cassie's car, this street, the separate cities they lived in, Jack had responsibilities. But right here, right now, nothing but opportunities. Waking up to a morning like this was sometimes indescribable, a morning like this could change a person and was what most people dreamed about. Today Jack was able to see and hold his future, the sounds of silence had never rung so loud.

As Jack's mind continued to wander, Cassie's impetuous eyes suddenly fluttered open. That look, that smile, the way she whispered "good morning" fractured his unassailable soul, supplying him with an undeniable peace. This was the routine they kept to and stuck with for many years. Nothing more, nothing less. The candor of Jack's little renegade was becoming difficult to handle. He never spoke the words he kept locked deep inside, never offered her more than she ever wanted or expected and this is why their relationship had lasted so long. Would she ever want more? He hoped someday she would.

Eventually Jack would have to take a chance and put all his cards on the table, he had to say what he kept hidden inside. He had to tell her that he loved her more than life itself, and he hoped she felt the same. Well, that day came and went, and unfortunately Cassie wasn't as receptive as Jack had hoped. Not long after that she declared it was time for her to move on, to figure out what direction her life would take, and she couldn't do that with him around. Just like that it had ended, all that was right was gone, and that was 30 years ago.

Well, about one year ago Jack woke from a dream he had about Cassie, the infamous elm tree, and their nights in her old Skylark. The exact time Jack woke from this dream—5:30 a.m., just as he had so many times when they were together. After a 29-year absence she had finally returned, at least in his dreams she had. Not knowing what to do next, Jack felt forced to return to the scene of the crime on Silvery Lane, no matter how much it may hurt.

As Jack drove to the spot where they spent so many innocuous nights, his hands started to sweat. Even his heart seemed to be afflicted. Moments later he arrived under the familiar tree. Except now he felt alone and conflicted, as a labyrinth of emotions shook Jack to his core, and Cassie, she wasn't in his life anymore.

Jack sat in his car for over an hour comparing how much the neighborhood had changed over the years. When in all likelihood it might have just been the brightness of the afternoon sun. He was getting ready to leave when a yellow truck pulled up onto the cobblestone driveway. The driver got out and went around to the back of his truck, pulled out a yellow "for sale" sign and stuck it in a pre-dug hole in the lawn between the bungalow and tree. A home, which Jack had barely noticed until now. Jack wondered what the view from inside might be like. So he reached for his phone, dialed the realtor's number and set an appointment for later in the week.

Today was now the big day. Jack filled out the big check, signed all the papers and collected the keys. After all that, he was finally the proud owner of a home and the tree that held so many fond memories. Standing on the porch holding the keys tightly. Jack couldn't help but think what Cassie's response might have been, if he had pulled onto the cobblestone drive and handed her these keys 30 years ago. Would she have accepted? Would she still have run? And why had she left in the first place? So many unanswered questions still lingered, and so far buying this new place hadn't helped to unravel that mystery.

Jack's plan for his first night would be to sleep in the master bedroom on a brand new king-size bed. Just him and his 4-year-old Husky named Sassy. What he was wishing was something altogether different: one more night under the stars in a black Buick and under a tree he now owned. A tree that sheltered them for years. A tree that stood the test of time, something he and Cassie had failed to achieve. As insignificant as it might seem to most, that elm was all he had left of her.

On that first night alone something happened, Cassie had once again returned to his dreams and did so every night for weeks on end. Jack woke every night at 5:30 a.m. sharp, just as he had so many years earlier. Maybe it was the birds, maybe it was something different. Maybe it was the thoughts of her that never seemed to leave. After several weeks, Jack started to think buying this place had been a huge mistake. For all these sleepless nights had started to take a toll on him both mentally and physically. Jack's boss at work had also taken notice of his lack of production. What could Jack do now? Should he try to locate Cassie? Did she want to be found? If he did find her, would she be willing to meet him? For Jack there was no right or wrong answer, only more questions. Still something had to be done.

Finally one Thursday after tossing and turning for more than three hours, Jack couldn't take it anymore. He jumped out of bed, put on his Crocs and a t-shirt, grabbed his car keys and said to his half sleeping dog, "Sass, are you coming?" The dog stood up, stretched, and slowly followed Jack down the hallway to the garage. When Jack reached the truck in the garage he opened the driver's door, and Sassy jumped in. Jack followed and closed the door of the blue F-150. Then he started the vehicle, hit the button to open the garage door, backed the truck out and parked I directly under the elm tree.

Sassy had been woken up and was ready to enjoy a ride elsewhere, anywhere; she didn't care. So when Jack turned the truck off, Sassy must have thought Jack had gone crazy. After several minutes of staring out the window, Sassy finally found a comfortable spot and laid her head on Jack's right thigh.

It was well after 2 a.m., the street was empty, a lone traffic light blinked red in the distance. Jack flipped through several stations hoping to find something to help him sleep. After failing to locate anything worth listening to, Jack pulled out *Purple Rain* and loaded it into the CD player. He then closed his eyes and tried to get comfortable in his reclined seat. Jack prayed for some real sleep, a sleep that would be the first since purchasing his own spot on Silvery Lane.

But at 5:30 a.m. Jack woke to an all too familiar sound, chirping birds, just as he had done three decades earlier. He rubbed his eyes, sat up, looked around; everything seemed the same as it had all those years before. To Jack it felt as though he had come back in time, the darkness returned him to a place he felt he never left. Looking into his rearview mirror something new was revealed, the grey in his beard, and the distinctive lines that stretched outward from the corners of his eyes which told Jack the truth about where he really was—alone!

Sassy started stretching on the front seat and looking around to see things for herself. About a minute later, Jack noticed a car parked near his rear bumper. He couldn't make out the brand, only that it was dark blue or black and seemed fairly new. The second thing Jack spotted was someone reclined in the car's driver's seat with what seemed to be blonde-colored hair. But he couldn't be sure because the glow from the car's radio didn't emit enough light.

Jack smiled, his mind raced, his heart seemed heavy. Was this a joke? Could it be the woman he longed for, for over half his life? Or was it just a coincidence? Maybe just a random stranger who happened to show up on his tailgate at this exact moment, or an answer to his prayers. Well, Jack had never been someone who believed in coincidences so he climbed from his truck as Sassy tagged along. The light from the truck seemed to stir the occupant in the car, which Jack could now see was a dark blue Buick less than one year old. When he reached the Regal's door the driver's window slowly rolled down. Jack could now clearly recognize his long lost nightingale sitting right there. The years had been kind—same hair, same blue eyes, same smile. She was beautiful.

As their eyes met Jack smiled and asked, "Is that my old shirt?" With a straight face Cassie answered, "Yes and why are you parked in my spot?"

Jack laughed out loud which startled the dog as she gave off a soft yelp. Cassie looked out toward the dog and asked, "Who's this?" "Oh this is Sassy, my best friend." Jack answered. "Sassy? You gave your dog the nickname you once gave me?" she questioned.

With a puzzled look Jack answered, "What did you expect me to do, talk to myself? Besides she's just as sassy as you ever were." Then Jack reached into the pocket of his sweats and fished out a solemn key from his key ring and tossed it to Cassie.

"What's this for?" She asked.

"The front door of that house, so we won't have to sleep in a car for the rest of our lives." Jack said slyly.

Cassie got out of the car, walked around to the passenger side rear door and opened it.

Jack asked, "What are you doing?"

"Getting your granddaughter," she answered.

"How is that possible?" He asked.

"That's why I left all those years ago, I was pregnant and didn't want to burden you. We were young, and you had big plans for the future. I didn't want you to regret your life. I have a daughter who is now 29, and this is her little girl, Shelby. She's 6 months old. Shelby couldn't fall asleep, so we went for a ride and ended up here."

Jack was astonished. He didn't know what to say or do. Cassie walked over to Jack holding the baby and asked, "Do you want to hold her?"

"I'd rather hold you first," Jack quipped. Then he put his arms around Cassie and hugged them both.

"Do you still love me?" She asked.

"Always!" Said Jack. "Oh, and what took so long getting here?"

Cassie just smiles and said, "I didn't have the address!"

Gary "SII" Studer II
Something New Every Day

It came to an end when the alarm started reporting on the Infiniti while I was waxing the hood and fender. That's when a strange squeaking or beeping—I thought it was the car alarm—woke me up. I sat up on my bunk and yawned, rubbing my eyes. The squeaky beeps paused for the moment it took for me to stretch. As I made my bed, the audible annoyance began again. Like it was aware my attention had subsided. It was then that I made the distinction that the beeps were that of a chirping bird.

I'm in prison, so there aren't any trees near my window. I finished making my bed and peered outside to investigate the bird's whereabouts. As I approached the window, the chirping stopped like the damn thing knew I was there, and it didn't want me to locate its position. I stared outside, surveying the landscape closely for several minutes—other buildings, picnic tables, the fence, no birds. I gave up the search and redirected my attention to my morning ritual. I put cream, sugar, and coffee in my mug, baited my toothbrush, slipped on my shower shoes, and made my way to the restroom. All while that bird maniacally sang his praise for... today?

I did my restroom thing, got hot water for my coffee, and headed to the microwave. In the dayroom, I ran into a guy I knew at another joint that just rode in. We caught up and bullshitted for a bit before we decided to meet up on the big yard after lunch.

I returned to my cube where three of my seven cubies still slept. I jumped on my rack, turned on my TV, and stacked my pillows so I could lay back on them. I sipped from my cup and switched the channel to ESPN so I could check the score of last night's game. I got the score, then switched to the warden's channel to look at the movie while I drank my mud and woke up. A picture of Amy Winehouse was on the screen, so I put in one of my earbuds and sat back against the pillows. The coffee called, so I took a couple more sips then sat down my cup. That's when the chirping resumed. I put in both earbuds to drown out the sound, but the incessancy bled through any silent second. I grabbed my cup and took another drink while the chirping continued. I took another gander outside, but still couldn't see any birds. It sounded like the son-of-a-bitch was perched atop my TV—it was so loud. So I looked. I had to laugh at myself. Am I losing it? Did a screw loosen while I slept? I know damn right there is not going to be a bird on my TV. Why'd I look?

I stretched back out on the pillows and glanced at the screen, enjoying the java for a couple minutes before I noticed the chirping had desisted. As annoying as it was, its absence left a sense of emptiness. Hell, I kinda missed it. Oh, well, the quaint subtlety that comes with quiet mornings in the pen is serene. The moment I began to settle with that concept, yep, "chirpchirpchirpchirpchirpchirp… " It was like he had something to say and couldn't say it loud—or fast—enough. I smiled at his effort. I looked again for this vociferous creature, but again, nothing. I observed the design of the other buildings to see if there was a sill above my window he could be on. The closest he could be was on the roof's edge which was at least five feet higher than the top of the window. I sat back, shaking my head, thinking, "I admire his tenacity, whatever his cause."

I saw "Footy" cover his head with his pillow as he said, "Shut that window." "H.P." answered from under his pillow, "It's shut." "Footy" queried with a snarl, "Is he in the damn cube?" I laughed and said "No, I checked. But he's pissed wherever he is." He replied, "He's bitchin' bout somethin', huh?" The chirping faded to a dull sound for a couple of minutes, then returned to a full blown alarm—like it was before. This continued for at least two more hours through count and before chow; loud as hell for a couple of minutes, then distant and quieter for a few. But almost constant. Maybe 10 minutes were undisturbed by the bird's noisy rant that whole time.

After chow, I put off meeting my "Greve" to further investigate this morning's disturbance. I could hear the continuous chirping as I approached the exterior of my building, but as I neared my window, it ceased. I noticed a darker area on the grass at the end of the building. I stepped closer, leaning in to see what it was. As I focused in, I realized it was a dead bird lying with its wings sprawled open. I heard a single "CHIRP" and looked up in the direction of the sound to see a bird on the roof of my building staring down at me with its head almost completely sideways. Then it flew away.

It was in that moment—through the bird—I realized my ability to empathize…

…I felt its pain.

Arianna Elisabeth Thomas
Food: A Memoir

The obsession with what I thought was my ideal weight started when I was 10 years old. My focus would be on controlling all aspects of food intake for many years.

I grew up with an African American father, Italian grandfather, and Polish grandmother. My grandmother was the main cook in the household. She would make homemade pierogies, stuffed cabbage, duck blood soup, crepes, and paczki on a regular basis. I was never a chubby kid because I was always active. My kindergarten teacher observed the fact that I was always hyper. My birth mother took me to a specialist who diagnosed me with ADHD and prescribed Ritalin. My relationship with food would change from that moment on.

When I took my Ritalin, I experienced two severe side effects. One, my nose would bleed on a daily basis. When I would experience a nose bleed, it would take an average of forty-five minutes to an hour to stop. And my appetite disappeared. My grandfather and grandmother had moved out when I started to lose my appetite. It was a struggle for me to eat anything. When I was at school, I would nibble like a rabbit and occasionally would eat a quarter of the food on the plate. My body weight was less than normal. My primary doctor sent me to the dietician at the age of 7. The vitamins and a special protein-rich diet were no help.

I attended St. Florian's School for the majority of middle school. I was the only biracial child in my class, and I was a loner. My teacher took a special interest in me. She realized that I was ahead of the majority of my class in most of the subjects. It was her conclusion that I did not need the Ritalin. The reason I would not pay attention in the classroom most of the time was boredom. My teacher's conclusions and the fact my mom lost her high-paying job and the health insurance led me to stop taking Ritalin. My appetite came back, and I started to gain weight. A classmate, Courtney, taught me how to starve myself and purge. I thought it was the solution to my problem.

I had a new daily routine. Saltine crackers, carrots, celery, and broccoli with a side of ranch dressing was my main diet during the weeks I would limit my intake of food. Sweets, chicken nuggets, and pizza were the foods I would eat during my purge weeks. An example would be when I would eat cookies and a slice of cheesecake and then would make myself throw up five to ten minutes later. The next step would be to brush my teeth right after. Courtney's sister would provide Courtney and me with a daily cocktail of diet pills. I got back to my goal weight of 110 pounds within six months of establishing this routine.

Self mutilation was the next habit I picked up. I would cut myself on my arms and legs with razors, keys, and pieces of glass. I would cut myself five to six times a week. Pain was my best friend and comfort.

When I was 14 years old, my classmate Valentina told my gym teacher she found a key with fresh blood on it. My mom took me to Children's Hospital the same day. The doctor gave my mom referrals to outpatient counseling centers. She never took me to any counseling center, so I continued the cycle of starving myself, purging, and self mutilation. I looked up the best foods to eat when you are on a starvation diet. I maintained honor roll status while devoting myself to essentially killing myself in a slow, painful manner.

High school arrived with a whole new set of challenges. My goal was to get into a good college and do as many activities as possible. I was also socializing with older men, so I had to maintain my cute figure. I purged my food five to six times a week at this point. I still cut myself five to six times a week.

When I was 15 years old, I was at a friend's house for a party. I was living on saltines, diet pills, and water this week in particular. All I remember is passing out and knocking my head against a granite countertop. One of the adults at the party rushed me to the hospital. The doctors discovered that I was malnourished and dehydrated. They discovered I had signs of the most common eating disorders, anorexia and bulimia, and scars from cutting for five years. The party was over at this point.

I finally went to a residential treatment center. The program lasted 60 days. The program saved my life. I was at my lowest weight of 96 pounds. I had a feeding tube in my nose so I could receive more nutrition. When I could eat real food again, it was like I was a baby all over again. There were foods that I had not eaten in years that my system had to learn to tolerate. The bathroom door inside my room was locked for the first 30 minutes after every meal so I could not throw up my food. The group meetings every morning were tough at first but became empowering towards the end.

There is an exercise that summed up my struggle with anorexia and bulimia. Each person had to draw themselves on a big white piece of paper. I had to mark where I thought every one of my flaws were. My fat thighs were always the one flaw I focused on. The group leader would then have each person explain why we felt that was a flaw and attempt to change our thinking. Fat on my legs was horrible. I told the leader I would exercise all day to get rid of the fat on my legs. Ms. Beth got me to realize that every woman has problem areas on their body. I needed to accept and love every problem area. We did this exercise once a week.

This exercise, over the course of two months, helped me realize that I can live with fat on my legs and hips. My self image improved once I realized that I would never be rail thin and that was okay.

I will always have a love and hate relationship with food. My solution for the past 13 years has been to eat healthy food, exercise on a daily basis in moderation, and participate in support groups to prevent a relapse. I have come to realize eating disorders are common among women and men of all races and ages. The key to winning a battle against an eating disorder is getting help.

If you notice that a friend or loved one is showing signs of an eating disorder, talk to them. When a person notices odd behavior, that talk is the first step to treatment. I am blessed to have won my battle because some people do not.

TimA
Ode to Ramen

Like many prison inmates I owe my very survival to your savory, salty goodness. The MRE of the penitentiary. You are always there when the chow hall lets me down to satisfy my hungry longing for sustenance.

Your noodley presence is the only constant in a place where no one knows what tomorrow may bring. More enduring than a bunkie, waiting patiently in my locker to be called upon in a time of need.

Honeybuns and bagels may come and go, but your pasta lasts forever. You never grow old or mold, having a half-life rather than a shelf life. Meant to be crushed yet you are indestructible. Immortality incarnate.

Haute cuisine you may not be, yet comfort food you are. A staple ingredient in every dish, the most versatile of wonder foods. You inspire me to new heights of cookery as master chef of the microwave.

Flavor is your claim to fame. Packets of hot spicy intensity or meaty mellowness that travel far and wide beyond the expectations of ordinary condiments, to lift the spirits of diners in desperate need of taste enhancement.

Your value transcends your caloric content to become the currency of the land. Exchanging hands to pay our debts, you wander far before you spend your last to insure that I will make it 'til the dawn.

Hail to the noodle!

Robert Tiran
Suicide Is My 401(k)

For someone serving life without the possibility of parole, suicide is a retirement plan. It is something that is not only considered by all "lifers," but invested in. Sure the chance of freedom exists, but that is like winning the lotto. And after decades playing the numbers, one loses resolve. The odds of winning become diminished by those around us dying after 20, 30, 40 years "in."

It is difficult to share such confessions and even more difficult to admit the frequency with which I invest. A future like mine turns into 25 years, and nothing changes; passing 30, and these fences become my only friends; 40 in sight, and all I have ever known has disappeared or died… these are the circumstances which push the condemned to invest in a lifer's 401(k).

Some years ago, I awoke like most mornings. I rose with the sun and spent the following minutes enjoying the silence that the morning brings. I got up, gathered my cosmetics, and headed to the end of the rock (hallway). The bathrooms in prison are small; there is little privacy, except for a small mop closet.

As I stood before a sink and brushed my morning breath away, I noticed in the mirror a glimmer of movement inside the closet behind me. The door was positioned so that I couldn't see much… just someone moving within the dim lighting of the mop closet. As I continued watching, a face appeared. The prisoner within was someone who lived a few doors down. He was only familiar in that I knew his name. It is not unusual at this time in the morning for someone to be inside of this closet gathering cleaning supplies. But what raised my attention was the moment our eyes met, an undeniable sense of fright washed over me and made a home in my throat.

In prison, a rule written in an invisible memorandum states that others' business is just that: their business. To involve oneself in others' affairs is to stroll the prison yard with a sign staked to my back, "please stab me." I have witnessed firsthand the consequences of this rule for violations much less than this.

But despite my imaginary guidebook, I stepped to one side to get a clearer view of the contents of this closet. I did this mainly not to pry, but for a more selfish reason: personal security. And as I stepped to the left, still peering in the mirror, I witnessed this man's affairs… a hangman's noose. In this moment I was faced with multiple realities. If I informed the officers, I would surely learn my lesson in breaking invisible rules. If I interceded directly, there was no telling what violence he may respond with. But the trump card dealt between these two futures… if I continued to do nothing, that skeleton would weigh too much.

So I slowly stepped in the doorway, and spoke his name as gently as I could. He turned from squaring his knot, and in a voice just above a whisper yet below conviction he said, "This is my 42nd year." My eyes responded that I completely understood. I asked him to try and think about things, possibly reconsider. He responded, "I have had 42 years of considering and no one left… "

I whispered with a hoarse voice as tears began to swell around my eyelids, "Please don't place this burden on me… this knowing." He stared at me for what seemed like minutes, turned from me, and began to untie the noose from his almost coffin. I asked him as he proceeded to leave if he would consider a favor… maybe speak to the prison shrink. He stopped, and without turning, he said, "Sure," but that she didn't "know what 42 years turned into."

I watched him that day, and a few hours after lunch, I saw him head over to healthcare. I spent the rest of the day wondering if he had really spoke to the shrink and then wondered what might my repercussions be when he got back his bearings. What path might he take in teaching me a lesson in other people's business?

When I awoke the next morning, it was the same as always. I rose with the sun and was then reminded of a possible looming lesson. I gathered my cosmetics, and headed to the bathroom to wash away my sleep. As I approached this man's door, it was impossible not to notice the yellow tape blocking the door. I then noticed stains on his doorstep in a color which I knew by instinct. He had made his decision, and decided it was time to cash in his options. He slit his wrists that evening while I slept, wrapped himself in his blanket and granted himself parole. Furthermore, he had placed a note on his desk asking his victims to forgive him… I wonder if they ever did. You see, in prison, it seems the only way to be forgiven is to finish one's conviction.

What scares me is not the fact that I consider such options or that they surface quite often. The terror which inserts paper cuts into my heart as decades pass is when this thinking turns from often to daily, what then? I am strong and resilient. I am dedicated to never again being the boy who applied pressure to the trigger of a firearm. The debt I feel about my mistakes holds such weight that I could never be him again. I seek forgiveness from those affected by my choices with every single breath. Yet in this place, in reality, forty or fifty years in handcuffs… what else exists but a lifer's 401(k)?

I hope that if I am ever ready to cash in my options, that I do not burden anyone with such a debt. To my knowledge he never told anyone about our conversation. I guess he decided that he had spared me the weight and burden of knowing by choosing a different route. He was wrong.

James Washington, III
A Conversation With Rehabilitation...

On February 7, 2000, I was sentenced to life without parole for a homicide I committed as a minor. That ignorant decision I made cost a young man his life. I can only imagine the pain I've caused his family. They can only imagine I'm still the same juvenile who sat in the courtroom deserving of a sentence to die in prison. Without any restorative justice opportunities available to either of us, his family and I have not had the chance to dialogue in person, if they would even be willing.

I'm ashamed, embarrassed, and very remorseful for my actions. Today, as a young man, I apologize again to his family and mine. The way I used to think had me blind to the full effects of my behavior. My perception of responsibility did not exist. My thinking made me believe I was right. Not that I actually was right, but it was the sum total of what I was taught by my family and the streets since I was 9 years old—as were my abuse of alcohol, tobacco, non-medical marijuana, and cocaine.

I know the natural inclination exists for society to expect the worst of juvenile lifers. Rightly so, since in my case a homicide was committed. As a consequence, this juvenile was not sentenced to a life of proper human development but life in prison without parole.

I am writing these words to speak for me and those of us who were adolescents, whose actions today prove the opposite of our worst yesterday. This does not make us blameless, but it shows that the potential for us to be productive members of society and deserving of a second chance has neither faded nor disappeared.

My name is James Washington, III. I am 34 years old, an involved father of two wonderful teenage daughters. I am also one of the many juvenile lifers incarcerated in Michigan. Today is my 6,266th day behind bars.

When I entered prison, I was a kid. There were no protective measures, extra concerns for my well-being, or separation from violent sexual predators. From day one as a juvenile with a life sentence in the Michigan Department of Corrections, no rehabilitative programs would be offered to me. Programs were only considered for and given to persons with the earliest release date. I have none.

Trying to understand this was confusing on a few levels. Now sober, I had to come to terms with taking a man's life, my life sentence, and learn to accept the fact that there would be no opportunities offered to me for help. To survive, my only option was to imitate what the other prisoners did on the yard.

The general population yard... the yard of loud talking, gang violence, fights, stabbings, exercising, the over-medicated, the under-medicated, gambling, sexual predators, narcotic use and abuse, bullying, tattooing, crying, bleeding, laughing, manipulation, razor-slashing, alcoholism, respectful/disrespectful officers, prejudiced/biased officers, officers who cared sometimes.

The distress led me to a conversation with rehabilitation. The funny thing is, Webster's only advice was the definition of the word. It wasn't much. Nor was I mature enough to see it as a starting point that could grow into an advantage.

Later, I was introduced to a man named Lil Joe. He was 52 years old and had been locked up over 24 years. I was 18. We agreed to work out together. From there we built a friendship that would ultimately grow into a father-and-son relationship, something I never had before. He taught me everything I needed to know about prison and about being a man. What I loved about him the most was he still valued the morals and principles his mother and father raised him with, and he never compromised since coming to prison.

A year later, I earned my first certificate of completion for "Custodial Maintenance Technology." I was 19. It was exciting earning something positive despite the obstacles of my sentence.

Joe underwent open heart surgery and returned to the prison rather fragile. It was hard for me to see him in that condition; even harder for me to stand by and watch him fight on the yard. Without a second thought, I jumped in. When it was over, I was cuffed and placed in the hole. It was my first misconduct ticket. I was found guilty of the assault, and after 40 days in segregation, I was transferred to a different prison. From December 2001 through July 2007, I received nine more tickets. Five of them landed me in seg. I was transferred amongts five other prisons. However, I managed to participate in a three-month class and received a certificate of completion for "Phase II Substance Abuse."

On July 2, 2007 I was found guilty and placed in seg for my 10th ticket for assaulting a prisoner. I have to admit, of all of the times I had been sent to the hole, this time was different. Three months prior, I spoke with my mother on the phone and was anticipating a visit from her for my 25th birthday. April tenth. A week passed but no visit. I was called to the prison's administration building. Through a service window with bars and a metal vent to speak through, an officer pushed a piece of paper to the ledge. All I could see was a blank piece of paper. He pressed it forward and pointed to a tiny sentence written at the bottom of the paper that read, "YOUR MOTHER IS DEAD." Under my breath I remember whispering to myself in shock... "What?" In that moment, a part of me died, too. "YOU CAN'T KEEP THE PAPER!" He screamed at me from behind the window. But in my mind I wanted to fight the paper! Then with the same attitude, he asked me, "Is you alright?!" What choice did I have? I learned how to deal with tragedies and grief by holding it in. The same way I saw my mother deal with it. Hours later, I was living in prison as if I'd never read the sentence. However, I *had* read that sentence. Little did I know, it would demand my attention, more than my strength, to suppress it.

There I was, sitting in the hole for my 10th misconduct ticket. Without warning, all my emotions came pouring out. Tears cascaded down my face like a spring waterfall. I cried for a lot of reasons. One, my mother was dead. Two, I wasn't there to help her at the end because I was locked up for life. And, three, I wasn't able to hold her hand when she breathed her last. The sense of loneliness I felt in the core of my being scared me.

That night I was forced to deal with my feelings, which was foreign to me. Yet, the more I cried, the more I found the strength to explore every emotion I had learned to suppress. Inside my pain, I could not help but think about all the pain I had caused others. And to think, if I felt this way about my mother, I felt the pain I caused my victim's family. He was someone's brother, father, uncle, and, like me, someone's son.

That night, I made a promise to myself and to God: I would not harm another person or do anything illegal ever again. And as my atonement to God for taking the life of another man, I would do my best to do enough good for *two* people. I did not know how this would look, feel, taste, or what it would sound like. I just knew deep down inside it was my only option.

I stepped out with faith in God, which led me to a study course given by Minister Louis Farrakhan titled, "Self Improvement: The Basis for Community Development," a 21-unit study guide designed to cause self-examination, self-analysis, and self-correction. Equipped with this knowledge, I was well on my way to a new life even though I was well aware I still lived behind metal bars and razor wire fences. Nevertheless, when I was released from segregation I grabbed my duffle bag and headed to my next cell, carrying my promise in my heart.

The last sentence I just wrote took place in my life NINE YEARS AGO. That was the last time a misconduct ticket was written on me. Today is August 28, 2016, and I am a mentor in two programs. The first is "Youth Deterrence." Once a month, at-risk teens are brought into the prison from Saginaw, surrounding counties and as far away as Kalamazoo, Michigan. They arrive from Saginaw High School, Arthur Hill High School,

Saginaw Juvenile Probation, Interlink Churches, Operation Reach, the Department of Human Services, and community organizations.

Contrary to "Scared Straight," we deter teens from engaging in criminal activity by showing them their true value. As a mentor, I tell my story candidly and without mincing words, which they easily relate to. By the time we divide into small groups, they are willing to have an open and honest dialogue about their specific issues and more. From there, we empower them with the tools necessary to take steps to change their lives. We end with a goal-setting action plan that shows how to practically achieve the goals they set for themselves. The program is so effective it has unified the most unlikely combination of people; prisoners working with Saginaw County's juvenile probation officers, police, prosecutors, judges, interns, and community leaders together saving children's lives.

The second program I mentor in is "Common Ground," a 14-week workshop within prison offered to those deemed trouble-makers or "the worst of the worst." We cover a wide range of common life skills (communication, character, values, conflict resolution, and parenting) that are uncommon to the mentees. As a mentor, I use my life's transition to show it is realistic and practical. Through these mentor programs, since 2012, we have changed the lives of hundreds of teens who were on the verge of throwing their lives away. Participating in these programs has been one of the most redeeming things I have ever done. I'm able to be for these at-risk teenagers what I wish someone had been for me.

Besides these mentor programs, I was blessed through a partnership with Central Michigan University (CMU), the professors who came into the prison, and seventeen honors students who were brought inside prison over a course of three months where we collectively engaged in a course of study titled, "Communication and Social Justice." The professors designed the course to help us mentors in our quest to better serve young people.

In 2011, before the CMU class and the two mentor programs, I was introduced to a Saginaw Valley State University (SVSU) professor. Under her tutelage for three years, I learned college-level literature. At the end of each semester she would invite her current class of SVSU students to come inside the prison to experience a combined class. All students always left with the excitement of having experienced one of the most engaging classes of the semester.

From these college classes I earned certificates of completion. I've also earned certificates from classes such as communication, anger management, Cage Your Rage, group counseling, music appreciation, introduction to playing the guitar, substance abuse, Inside Out Dad, biohazard clean up, and basic conversational Spanish.

Before any of these productive experiences entered my life, I remember having a conversation with rehabilitation. But Webster only provided me the definition of the word. Today, not only am I mature enough to see it as a starting point that grew into a promise, I see very clearly my life is an example of the word.

Authors' Statements

Please note that Authors' Statements are published in those cases where statements were available/present.

Missie Alanis

I am a black female, but I am hated and loved equally by my own race, who are being killed outside and inside these gates by the government. Black lives matter, but somehow LGBTQIA don't? Orlando really got to me; I would not have sent this second letter out if the inspiration for this meaningful work hadn't been there. Angels guided my hand on this one 49 of them, that's 98 wings to carry every word right to you. At least I can give this poem to them and their loving memories of what was and could have been. Every life matters!

Jennifer Avery

I've been writing poetry since I was a preteen, and I will continue until I'm no longer part of this world. Living in a very unstable environment can take its toll on our past mistakes, but it's up to each of us to work through them and rehabilitate ourselves in a more productive manner. I've seen a lot in my years of life, but through my poetry, I'm not a product of that… I'm a writer. "Hollow House" is a sad version of what was my reality dealing with an illness that led to my conviction.

Craig Benson

Undoubtedly I am in love with the entire process of writing and especially poetry. Since I was not lucky enough to be given a classical education, few are these days, I am only now learning these skills. "I Told You So!" is a short story I came up with after I was given these chicken pictures. Maybe a bit of political satire? I Just love to write odd stories and Aesop-style fables with my own personal twists.

Charles G. Brooks, Sr.

I am the father of black children in America. I am an incarcerated black man. There is an unrelenting onus for me to share my perspective, not only with my children, but with whomever cares to read what I write. The words on these pages are my escape. They are every tool I can bring to bear, in order to teach the lessons that aren't taught in the classrooms of America. I am an advocate of universal unity, and hope that by shining a light on my inner issues, the children I love will reap the benefits. The world, at large, will gain an improvement. If you like any of my work, feel free to get Free Thoughts, Incarcerated Man, available at www.amazon.com.

Demetrius Buckley

I commend all inmate writers for creating in such a tumultuous environment. It takes a certain amount—beyond normal amount—of will-power to blink in and out of reality to harmonize with chaos, to give discords balance... My adoration goes to you, the writer, & my thanks to PCAP for this avenue to show readers beyond that normal amount we willfully blink into...

John S. Copeman

This year and the year before have been very productive for me, now that I'm motivated to write and have a creative outlet to do so. I do. Everyday as a writer must. It is also important to remember NOT to get discouraged when churning out crap. Everyone does; it's all part of the process, and to quote Coolidge, "Nothing in the world can take the place of persistence." So keep moving that pen and sooner or later you'll mine a nugget or two. Writers read, think, write and erase. And re-write some more.

James Galt

Prison strips you of many things. You lose family, friends and loved ones, and, obviously, the freedom to perform the multitude of tasks that people on the outside take for granted. Being denied so much, you learn to make do with what you actually need—your basic requirements—and can derive spiritual strength from surviving on such minimal resources. Much of my writing comes from this pared-down, yet hopeful, version of myself.

Monica Givens

Hello, my name is Monica, and I am a 35-year-old mother of two, who also happens to be in prison. My life has not been easy. I've had great struggles, more than my share of pain, and made some extremely poor choices. I do not let these things define me; however I do not shy away from them—I write about them. If even one person can relate or learn from my experiences, then it wasn't all in vain.

Maine Harrell

A woman needs to be appreciated. A nation can rise no higher than its women. A woman goes through a lot, and we live in a society that does not really appreciate the sanctity of birth and does not encourage the woman to get in touch with her feelings. Pregnancy is measured socially, and it is either acceptable or not, depending upon the circumstances of the moment. In fact, a growing fetus in the womb cannot distinguish between feelings the mother has toward others and the feelings she has toward the fetus. Whatever your mother experienced emotionally while pregnant, you took it personally. In the scriptures, God told Jeremiah the Prophet, "I knew you before you were in your mother's womb." This means your existence transcends the condition of your parents. The first week after the sperm met the egg, what were you experiencing? You took your journey down through the fallopian tubes, made contact with the lining of the womb. You connected with your mother, and if she did not want to be pregnant, you experienced your first trauma. The first attachment we experience is as a fertilized egg clinging to the wall of the womb, where our need to be made secure first manifests. You made that attachment successful. So many new life cells never made it. Some made it and were unable to hold on (miscarriage); worse, some were pulled away by an external force (abortion). No matter what your mother was feeling, she carried you to term. She went to the door of death itself to deliver you. Whether she did it willingly or unwillingly, she served as an agent of the Creator himself and brought you here.

D.L. Hemphill

My name is Daniel Hemphill ,and I am into year nine of a 31-year sentence. I started learning to express myself through writing about three years ago, and I am proud to say that my novel *Crayons-N-Bullets* has been published and is available on amazon.com.

I originally started writing my short story, "Another Day in Prison," to show my family what a day in prison is *really* like. When I let a few close friends read it, they were astounded by its accuracy and urged me to submit it to your contest.

Yolanda Hobson

My name is Yolanda; friends and family call me YaYa. I am currently in Huron Valley Corrections. I'm up for parole in February 2018. I am trying to pursue a career as a writer; it's a positive outlet. It has helped me heal and accept the things that have taken place in my life. So I hope you enjoy the poetry enclosed because it reflects on my life and how much I have grown and overcome it.

Blaque Sheet Ja

I got the name Blaque Sheet Ja from an associate of mines. Every time he would see me, I was always writing something, a book, poem, song, whatever comes to my mind. Through the years of my life I've grown to be a rebel. From parents passing at eight (father) and fifteen (mother), I was always defensive because I was always on my own. The poems I've chosen explain me all around. I'm from Detroit's Westside. I'm twenty-five years old. I started writing poetry after my pops died, but I never took it serious until my words started making me feel better. I call my style "Mixed Soul" because whatever the heart feels the pen tells. Poetry and writing is all I have left to love, so my passion will burn for eternity. Enjoy. Peace.

Asia Johnson

Spiritual awakenings, epic discoveries, life changing epiphanies, people finding themselves—for what seems like an eternity, I've envied the stories of people who had experienced such enlightenment. For 30 years I searched through the pitch black of night, lost and never found. But this year, my 30th year, my search for truth ended. It is through my writing that I not only find truth, but I speak it; I embrace it. My truth. T.S. Eliot said it is "not the assertion of truth, but the making of that truth more fully real to us."

The connection I feel to myself when I write cannot be described. It is a feeling that cannot be told or shown. But even as amazing as that connection is, the connection I feel to every single person who might read and be moved by my truth—that feeling of connection is life-giving.

Cameron Kelly

About myself: I'm a painter mostly who enjoys reading and writing songs. These are my first submitted pieces. I also enjoy time to myself and listening to music.

Ko

I believe in God. And ever since I was an adolescent, I thought that the future and futuristic technology were cool and something that I wanted to experience. So being that these are two of my favorite topics (God and the future!), I put the two together in a hip-hop song that I wrote called "Advancement." It is named so because the concept takes place in the year 2716. Not only is technology very advanced, but human beings are spiritually advanced as well. Through worship of God!

Dell Konieczko

Fifty-five now. Still living, still trying.

Randall Kuipers

What has shaped me? When did I choose a path less-travelled, and how has it affected me? Walk with me a while, as I share some of my choices, some of the different roads my life has followed. Some of these may be highways, heavy with traffic; others, country roads, or trails of dirt. I cannot see what traffic a road has carried, cannot gauge its congestion while traveling on it. But I can ask of those who also travel and of those who have gone before—can ask if they, too, have walked that road, or know of those who have—or if I am the first and only. Consider these, then, and respond with hand or thought if the way feels familiar. Maybe we are fellow travellers: five children * comic book collector * inmate * artist * crash survivor * bagpipe fan * a decade with one employer * two decades married to the same person * agnostic / secular humanist * cancer survivor * I believe in equal rights for all people, regardless of gender, race, or preference * I believe in finding beauty in all things * I believe that love is meant to be shared

Steven T. Lake

"My wife she cries on the barrack-gate, my kid in
      the barrack-yard.
It ain't that I mind the Ord'ly-room—it's *that* that
      cuts so hard.
I'll take my oath before them both that I will sure
      abstain,
But as soon as I'm in with a mate and gin, I know
      I'll do it again!"
                                    —Rudyard Kipling

Kyree Lyn

A 30-year-old Christian woman, with a checkered past in which much of my writing comes from. I have two sets of parents, three siblings, and four nieces that encourage me in every aspect of my life. Thank God for creativity and the will to carry it out.

Christopher Marek

Some writers make their mistakes in ink; I, unfortunately, have made many of my mistakes in real life—but I hope that chapter is coming to a close. I'm from Michigan's thumb. I'm serving time for multiple counts of safe-breaking, and I look forward to new beginnings.

Justin Monson

Justin Monson is a writer and visual artist currently located in Saginaw, Michigan. His work has appeared in volumes 6, 7, and 8 of the *Michigan Review of Prisoner Creative Writing*; in the literary journal *Duende*; and on the *Pacifica Literary Journal*'s website, as a finalist for their "Contest Without Form." He is currently working on a collection of poems based on his recent and ongoing experiences in love, waves, light beams, and vapors.

Jill Miller

When asked to write something positive about myself, I sat looking at the paper as if it would crumble into pieces if I touched it. I was stuck. Then after really searching myself, I thought back to my 39 years of life thus far… "It can't be all that bad, can it?" No … it's not; it wasn't. I began to jot down memories, stories—good and bad—and so formed this piece.

Every line, every phrase, has a story… most good. But it's *all* me, who I am, what made me the person I am today. I had a bump in the road on my crazy journey and ended up here, in this prison. But as I search who I am and where I am from, I'm finding the real me, the me I'm proud to be, the me I'm proud to go out and show my family and friends. I just pray that everyone will be able to look past my bump.

Marcellus Earl Phillips

Nice to see you again, this year, Wolverine writing fans. Trust me, it is my pleasure that you've invited me into your attentions. I am a burgeoning author. I've put any larger projects on hold to practice my craft with shorties and focus on group therapeutic endeavors as I speed into my season of parole eligibility. Thank you for caring and lending a little of your precious entertainment moments to us. Here's to better tomorrows than yesterdays.

Deyon Neal

Deyon Neal was born and raised in Detroit, Michigan. He received a 32-62 year sentence in the year 2000, when he was 19 years old. He discovered his passion for writing in prison and hopes that his stories inspire at-risk youth to change their lives for the better.

James Stevenson

The inspiration for this story came from a dream I had. It's about two people who spent many years apart though it seems they were together more than they knew. The story could have been longer and more detailed, but then the reader would not have had to search within for answers from their life experiences. We all need love and miss it when it's not part of our lives. This story is about something I miss.

Gary "SII" Studer II

The only things real about the story are that I'm in prison and the cube setting—and then the names. One of my cubies, "Cowboy," is a bit of an artist who makes cards. He asked me to draw with him, and this is what I drew.

Michael Sullivan

It has been a rough year for me. Here is this year's output.

Robert Tiran

My status as a criminal seems always to enter a room before I do, infecting any true introduction. Thus, explaining who I am is difficult due to who I was. I have regretfully discovered that the greatest mistakes are eternal, and this fact of forever ruins any meaningful... *nice to meet you.* So I will allow my words to speak for me and hope that you found them honest.

G WAHID

Peace!
"It's beautiful. The pain is beautiful, once you go through." My name is Glenn Rayshaw Bradley, and I go by the pen name of G Wahid, which stands for Glenn the Unique One. I've been writing seriously for about three years now. I have written a total of five books; *Battle Cries 1 and 2*, *The 7th of December*, *Giah's First Job*, and *I Can't Wait Until My Daddy Comes Home*. I've had a few articles published in a magazine in Brooklyn, New York, called *Spotlight on Recovery*. I write because it's cleansing to the soul. Writing has finally given me a voice in the world in which I would hope to make a positive impact. I dedicate my works to my beautiful sister Yunique Moss who is my biggest inspiration.

Charles Washington

When I first wrote this poem, Chachie was 6 years young. Every year that goes by I update his age in the poem. At the time of this writing, the year is 2004, and he is 18. This poem was emotional for me when I wrote it, and it is emotional for me every time I read it. As a result, I don't read it that much anymore. It was painfully written for Chachie during my incarceration. I had intended to write poems for my daughters Candice and Shanetta also, but it was too painful to do. I abandoned the idea. But I love them equally as much.

Calvin Westerfield

In prison, time and loneliness are both sadistic terrorists who have no aim or cause in their destruction, so I write. Life should be written about as it is experienced and done so creatively—this is my goal. Poetry is the only freedom I know, and it waits to escape from the tip of my pen, seeking a discerning eye or an attentive ear that will appreciate the emotions of my soul dwelling in the presence of ideas.

Fred Williams

Poetry, my poetry is a tool attempting to fix a broken system. I speak against mass incarceration, poverty, oppression, and sexism with intentions of gaining solidarity in the fight to deconstruct these horrid realities.

Greg Winer

Since a poem expressing sadness or sorrow for one who is dead is an elegy, I consider myself to be an elegist. After losing someone special to me, very suddenly and tragically, I have found expressing my sorrow through poetry to be quite therapeutic. While I have written many of these simple elegies, all relative to death, it is only now that I choose to begin to share them. I thank you.

A Word About the Prison Creative Arts Project

The Prison Creative Arts Project (PCAP) is an organization that opens up opportunities to create original works of art in correctional facilities, juvenile facilities, and urban high schools across the state of Michigan.

Founded in 1990, PCAP is run by members of the University of Michigan and surrounding community and is based in the University of Michigan Department of English Language and Literature. Its programs include the Annual Exhibition of Art by Michigan Prisoners, the largest prison art show in the world; The Michigan Review of Prisoner Creative Writing, the amazing collection of writing you are currently holding in your hands; weekly theatre, creative writing, visual art, and music workshops with incarcerated adults and juveniles, as well as students from Detroit; the Linkage Project, which affirms the creativity of adults and youth returning from incarceration; and the Portfolio project, a one on one collaboration between a volunteer and an incarcerated individual to create a portfolio of his or her best work.

The Prison Creative Arts Project's mission is to collaborate with these populations to strengthen our community through creative expression. We believe that everyone has the capacity to create art. Art is necessary for individual and societal growth, connection and survival. It should be accessible to everyone. The values that guide our process are respect, collaboration in which vulnerability, risk, and improvisation lead to discovery and resilience, persistence, patience, love and laughter. We are joined with others in the struggle for social justice, and we make possible spaces in and from which the voices and visions of the incarcerated can be expressed.

To learn more about PCAP, or to donate to our organization, please visit www.prisonarts.org.

CPSIA information can be obtained
at www.ICGtesting.com
Printed in the USA
FFOW05n0046060317

9 780998 647913